Grades 2-4

CHARACTER EDUCATION

INSTRUCTION · ACTIVITIES · ASSESSMENT

Published by World Teachers Press®

www.worldteacherspress.com

Order Number 2-5264
ISBN 978-1-58324-241-4

E F G H I 13 12 11 10 09

395 Main Street
Rowley, MA 01969
www.didax.com

Character Education

Character Education introduces and develops the knowledge, skills, attitudes and values that will help students lead healthy and fulfilling lives. Students will consider what it means to be healthy—socially, mentally and emotionally—and will be given experiences to assist them to become responsible, caring members of society.

The book focuses on character building and values. Most experts agree that people with defined values and a good self-image are better equipped to deal with challenging situations. The activities encourage students to consider their own values and develop a sense of self-worth. It also focuses on the importance of showing respect for and tolerance towards others and valuing diversity in our society.

Character Education provides a comprehensive coverage of values content, supports teachers in planning and implementing lessons and, through collaborative learning and thoughtful discussion, promotes a lifelong commitment to a healthy value base.

> **Other titles in this series:**
>
> *Character Education, Grades 4-6*
>
> *Character Education, Grades 6-8*

Contents

Teacher information

Character Education focuses on character building and values. The activities encourage students to consider their own values and develop a sense of self-worth. It also focuses on the importance of showing respect and tolerance towards others and valuing diversity in our society.

The notes on the following pages provide comprehensive information about terms and concepts used in this book.

A teacher notes page accompanies each student worksheet. It provides the following information:

Specific indicators explain what the students are expected to demonstrate through completing the activities.

Background information has been included to enhance your understanding of the concept being taught and to provide additional information to relate to the students.

Discussion points have been suggested to further develop ideas on the student worksheet. They can also encourage the students to comprehend, assess and form opinions about what they have read.

What to do gives suggested step-by-step instructions for the activity. The accompanying worksheet may be the focus of the activity or it may be where the students record their ideas after completing a task or discussion.

Answers to all worksheet activities are included. Some answers will need a teacher check, while others will vary depending on the students' personal experiences, opinions, etc.

Additional activities can be used to further develop the outcomes being assessed. These activities provide ideas to consolidate and clarify the concepts and skills taught in the activity.

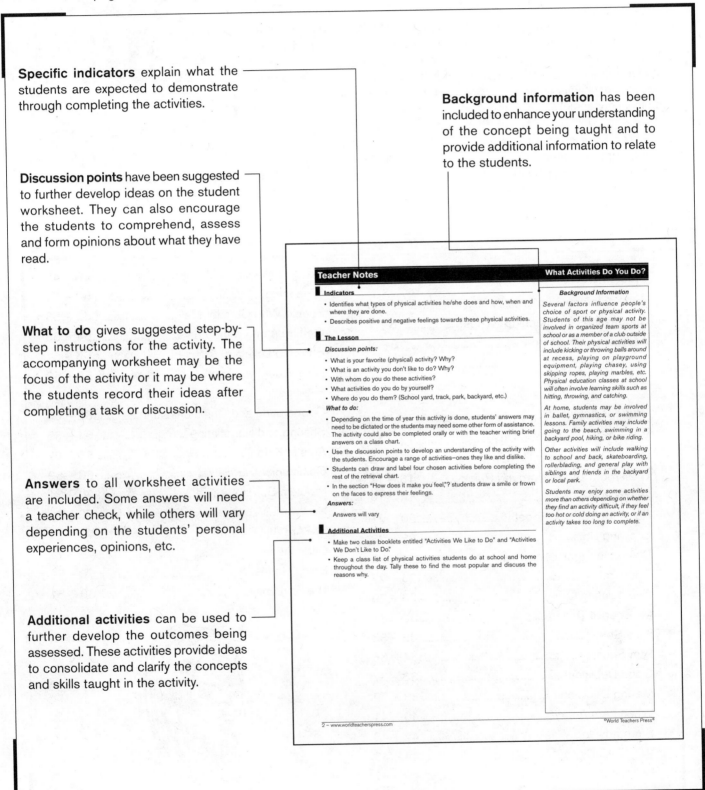

Teacher Notes — What Activities Do You Do?

Indicators

- Identifies what types of physical activities he/she does and how, when and where they are done.
- Describes positive and negative feelings towards these physical activities.

The Lesson

Discussion points:

- What is your favorite (physical) activity? Why?
- What is an activity you don't like to do? Why?
- With whom do you do these activities?
- What activities do you do by yourself?
- Where do you do them? (School yard, track, park, backyard, etc.)

What to do:

- Depending on the time of year this activity is done, students' answers may need to be dictated or the students may need some other form of assistance. The activity could also be completed orally or with the teacher writing brief answers on a class chart.
- Use the discussion points to develop an understanding of the activity with the students. Encourage a range of activities–ones they like and dislike.
- Students can draw and label four chosen activities before completing the rest of the retrieval chart.
- In the section "How does it make you feel,"? students draw a smile or frown on the faces to express their feelings.

Answers:

Answers will vary

Additional Activities

- Make two class booklets entitled "Activities We Like to Do" and "Activities We Don't Like to Do."
- Keep a class list of physical activities students do at school and home throughout the day. Tally these to find the most popular and discuss the reasons why.

Background Information

Several factors influence people's choice of sport or physical activity. Students of this age may not be involved in organized team sports at school or as a member of a club outside of school. Their physical activities will include kicking or throwing balls around at recess, playing on playground equipment, playing chasey, using skipping ropes, playing marbles, etc. Physical education classes at school will often involve learning skills such as hitting, throwing, and catching.

At home, students may be involved in ballet, gymnastics, or swimming lessons. Family activities may include going to the beach, swimming in a backyard pool, hiking, or bike riding.

Other activities will include walking to school and back, skateboarding, rollerblading, and general play with siblings and friends in the backyard or local park.

Students may enjoy some activities more than others depending on whether they find an activity difficult, if they feel too hot or cold doing an activity, or if an activity takes too long to complete.

Character Education–Book 1

A variety of student worksheets is provided, which may contain a selection of role-plays to perform; scenarios to read and consider; information to read, discuss and answer questions about; or values or feelings to consider and compare with others.

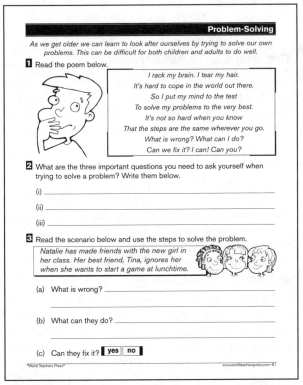

Student activities to reinforce and develop understanding of the concept.

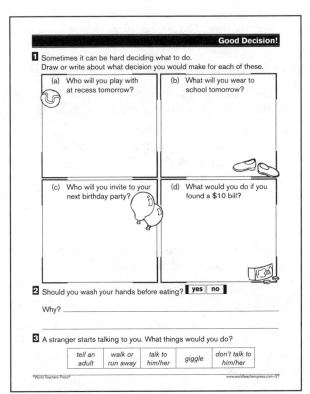

Questioning activities where students are required to consider and evaluate personal feelings or values.

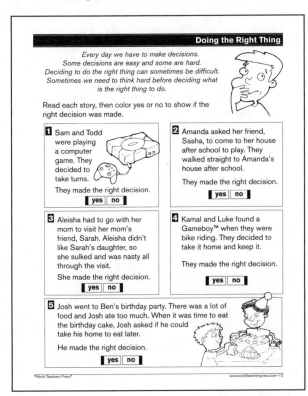

Several pages provide a selection of role-plays or scenarios for students to use in a variety of ways.

Other activities include completing tables or reading and labeling diagrams.

Suggestions for Teaching Character Education

Character Education introduces and develops the knowledge, skills, attitudes and values that will enable students to lead healthy and fulfilling lives. Students will consider what it means to be healthy—socially, mentally and emotionally—and will be given the tools to become responsible, caring members of society.

Many of the activities in this book provide students with an opportunity to formulate their thoughts on a topic and express their opinions and feelings. Classroom discussions are valuable for encouraging critical and reflective thinking.

Teaching Character Education

- Create a safe atmosphere in the classroom so students feel they can share their thoughts and feelings.

- Identify what it is the students are going to take away from the lesson. (Refer to the "Indicator" in the Teacher Notes for each activity.)

- Begin with a discussion or, with older students, a hypothetical situation. (Refer to the "Discussion points" in the Teacher Notes for each activity.)

- Listen to and be honest with the students. (Give something of yourself. Share some of your own experiences, where appropriate.)

- Show respect for the students' thoughts and feelings.

- Be non-judgmental.

In your responses, encourage students to analyze their statements by asking such things as "What could happen if you did that?" or "Who else would be affected by that?" rather than giving your own opinion.

With some topics, students may make suggestions where you can respond "Is that the RIGHT thing to do?" Such a question can promote discussions regarding individual, group, community, and global values. Who is it "right" for?

Although students should feel free to express their opinions, it is important that they understand there is a "right" conclusion, rather than letting them think whatever they conclude is correct.

Creating a Safe Atmosphere

For an effective values lesson to take place, students need to feel comfortable enough to share their thoughts, feelings, opinions and past experiences. They need to feel there will be no ridicule, no put-downs and a non-judgmental atmosphere.

One way to promote this safe atmosphere during discussions with younger students is to make the effort to sit the students in a circle, even if it means going to another room to do this. Some schools call this time "circle time." Set clear rules, such as one student speaking at a time and no put-downs or making faces. Make the circle a safe place where the students feel comfortable to talk openly about their feelings, worries and achievements.

Students can be encouraged to become respectful listeners. Ensure that students raise their hands if they wish to make a comment, or, for younger students, an item can be placed in the middle of the circle such as a "talking stick" or small toy. Only students holding this are able to speak.

Explain to the class that many people only "half listen" because they are thinking about what they might say when the speaker stops. Some people don't even wait for the speaker to stop, and interrupt him or her in the middle of a sentence. During "circle time," teachers and students have the opportunity to share their thoughts without being interrupted.

It is important for students to understand that personal issues discussed during these open forum meetings are not to become topics of conversation outside the classroom. You will also need to show respect to the students unless, of course, issues are raised involving abuse or that need attention by parents. You will then need to consult his/her principal regarding any action that needs to be taken.

Once the class has a routine set in place to discuss issues openly and respectfully, these skills can be transferred to discussions about issues affecting the class, such as conflict and bullying.

Suggestions for Teaching Character Education

Values Education

Most definitions agree that "values" are those qualities which an individual or a society considers to be important as principles for conduct.

The *Character Education* series helps students to consider their personal strengths and weaknesses and reinforces the advantages of having a strong set of values.

A person's set of values affects his or her thinking and behavior. When people are confident in themselves and have strong values, it is easier to do things that are "right." Those who have weaker values can often be led easily and may do things they don't really want to do.

You can encourage students to have a positive self-image through praise and by recognizing individual achievements.

You can foster the development of personal qualities such as perseverance, kindness, and dealing with stress and criticism. You can also discuss some values with students, such as honesty, generosity and tolerance. You might also like to discuss other things people value, like pets, music and the environment.

Tolerance and Empathy

Tolerance and empathy should be encouraged in students. Activities such as drama games, which require students to put themselves in someone else's place and imagine how that person feels, can help to foster empathy. Tolerance is an ongoing process that teaches students not to hate. You can teach tolerance most effectively by modeling tolerant behavior in the classroom and on the playground, ensuring students are exposed to multicultural literature and images, and teaching them about various faiths, ethnicities and lifestyles. Educating students to be tolerant will:

- promote the understanding and acceptance of individual differences.

- promote the idea that differences can enhance our relationships and enrich our society.

- minimize generalizations and stereotyping.

- promote the need to combat prejudice and discrimination.

This book emphasizes the importance of respecting the feelings and emotions of others. It uses scenarios to help students "put themselves in the shoes" of others. When students develop empathy for others, the dynamics of situations can change.

Collaborative Learning

When students are able to work together in groups, they are encouraged to communicate and express their ideas. It is important that you monitor groups working independently to ensure that all students are working together as a team. By assigning a role for each group member, it is more likely that the dynamics will be equitable. The roles of the students can be swapped regularly to give each member the opportunity to participate in all tasks.

Allow time at the end of the group tasks for the students to evaluate their team skills and to make targets to work towards the next time they form as a group. Some activities may work better if the groups are organized by ability levels, others will be enriched by mixed-ability groupings. To enable all students to work together at some stage during the year, randomly select groups for some activities.

Differentiating Activities

The activities in the *Character Education* series have been designed so they can be followed precisely or adapted by teachers. This flexibility allows you the opportunity to modify lessons and worksheets to meet the needs of students with varying abilities and special needs.

To meet the special needs of English as a second language (ESL) students or those who have low levels of literacy, plan a time to introduce keywords and concepts. Having other adult support is ideal as the group can work in a quiet area away from the classroom. Keywords can be enlarged and discussed. Being immersed in the language before a topic begins gives these students an advantage, especially during the teacher discussion part of the lesson, when most teachers tend to speak quite quickly.

If other adults are not available, mixed-ability groups will allow ESL students and students with low literacy levels to observe and be guided by other students.

Students who seem to "race" through the activities and worksheets and who understand the content very quickly can be challenged by looking at the topic in greater depth (rather than being given more of the same). They can go beyond the facts and conduct research related to strands of the topics that interest them.

By meeting the needs of individual students, allowing the students to learn collaboratively, and by having very clear instructions and expectations, values lessons should run smoothly.

Assessment Indicators

Below are the indicators from the activity pages of *Character Education, Grades 2-4*. These indicators can be transferred across to the assessment form on page 10. By using forms, you can meet the needs of outcome-based learning experiences in values education. The format of each page is ideal for inclusion in student portfolios or for reporting purposes. Using forms allows you to provide a well-explained, logically-presented indication of progress to both students and parents. Indicators have been developed as a basis for determining progress towards achieving outcomes.

Pages 12 – 13
- Identifies what types of physical activities he/she does and how, when and where they are done.
- Describes positive and negative feelings towards these physical activities.

Pages 14 – 15
- Identifies independent living skills.
- Expresses feelings about exercise and friendships.
- Identifies aspects about himself/herself which develop self-esteem.

Pages 16 – 17
- Identifies and illustrates rules appropriate for the classroom and the playground.
- Identifies reasons for having rules.
- Recognizes his/her responsibility to keep himself/herself safe by obeying rules.

Pages 18 – 19
- Identifies rules appropriate for home.
- Identifies reasons for having rules.
- Recognizes his/her responsibility to keep himself/herself safe by obeying rules.

Pages 20 – 21
- Matches pictures to appropriate rules.
- Writes a rule appropriate to a situation in a picture.

Pages 22 – 23
- Identifies activities relevant to a particular age.
- Identifies ways to help at home and at school.

Pages 24 – 25
- Selects right and wrong decisions.
- Illustrates scenarios appropriately.

Pages 26 – 27
- Identifies situations where children are cooperating.
- Identifies ways of cooperating.

Pages 28 – 29
- Identifies actions which show appreciation.
- Follows rules to play a game.

Pages 30 – 31
- Identifies people and things who/that are special to him/her.

Pages 32 – 33
- Identifies things he/she is good at to develop positive feelings of self-worth.

Pages 34 – 35
- Reads a poem about individuality.
- Identifies specific aspects which make him/her unique.

Pages 36 – 37
- Differentiates between important and unimportant decisions.
- Makes decisions based on positive and negative consequences.

Pages 38 – 39
- Identifies people who make specific decisions.
- Retells a good and a bad decision.

Pages 40 – 41
- Recognizes situations that make him/her angry.
- Identifies ways to deal with anger.

Pages 42 – 43
- Identifies strengths and weaknesses.
- Relates feelings about attempting new things.

Pages 44 – 45
- Identifies bullying situations in a variety of scenarios.

Pages 46 – 47
- Identifies bullying situations.
- Identifies strategies to cope with bullying situations.

Pages 48 – 49
- Identifies with the feelings of someone being bullied.
- Understands strategies to use if he/she is bullied.

Pages 50 – 51
- Identifies qualities which maintain good relationships.
- Completes a crossword about maintaining friendships.

Pages 52 – 53
- Identifies family members and how he/she is cared for by them.
- Identifies other people who care for them.

Pages 54 – 55
- Identifies skills used for getting along with other people.
- Identifies that not all interpersonal skills are used for all people.

Pages 56 – 57
- Identifies actions which show love and respect.
- Matches actions to specific people.

Pages 58 – 59
- Identifies feelings experienced in particular situations.

Pages 60 – 61
- Identifies feelings for a given situation.
- Identifies situations which evoke particular feelings.

Pages 62 – 63
- Identifies ways of cooperating and communicating effectively.

Assessment Indicators

Pages 64 – 65
- Completes an acrostic about sharing.
- Completes a word search using "negotiation" words.

Pages 66 – 67
- Discusses and identifies ways to be kind to others.
- Identifies feelings associated with being kind to others.
- Plans and follows through with an act of kindness towards a peer.

Pages 68 – 69
- Completes a news-telling plan.
- Evaluates listening skills.

Pages 70 – 71
- Identifies information about problem-solving steps from a poem.
- Uses problem-solving steps to solve a problem.

Pages 72 – 73
- Identifies events that cause stress or worry.
- Identifies activities that combat stress and aid relaxation.

Pages 74 – 75
- Identifies what makes him/her different from other people.
- Surveys and records information about his/her friends to show differences.
- Discusses the importance of valuing differences among people.

Pages 76 – 77
- Identifies differences and similarities among people.

Pages 78 – 79
- Identifies what it means to be trustworthy.
- Discusses what it means to be honest.

Pages 80 – 81
- Describes how to care for the environment.

Using the Assessment Form (page 10)

An explanation of how to use the form.

Task(s)
- Give a brief description of the activity and what was expected of the students.

Assessment
- Write the relevant indicator(s) as listed above and assess appropriately.

Teacher Comment
- Use this space to comment on aspects of an individual student's performance which cannot be indicated in the formal assessment, such as work habits or particular needs or abilities.

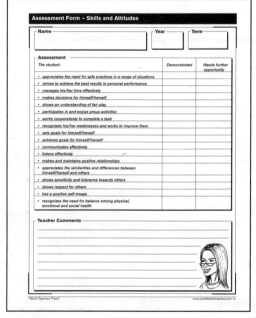

Using the Skills and Attitudes Assessment Form (page 11)

An explanation of how to use the form.

Assessment
- Assess the specific development of an individual student in these areas.

Teacher Comments
- Use this space to comment on an individual student's skills and attitudes.

Assessment Form

Name

Grade

Term

Task(s)

The student was asked to:

Assessment

The student:

	Demonstrated	Needs further opportunity

Teacher Comments

Assessment Form – Skills and Attitudes

Name

Grade

Term

Assessment

The student:	Demonstrated	Needs further opportunity
• appreciates the need for safe practices in a range of situations		
• strives to achieve the best results in personal performance		
• manages his/her time effectively		
• makes decisions for himself/herself		
• shows an understanding of fair play		
• participates in and enjoys group activities		
• works cooperatively to complete a task		
• recognizes his/her weaknesses and works to improve them		
• sets goals for himself/herself		
• achieves goals for himself/herself		
• communicates effectively		
• listens effectively		
• makes and maintains positive relationships		
• appreciates the similarities and differences between himself/herself and others		
• shows sensitivity and tolerance towards others		
• shows respect for others		
• has a positive self-image		
• recognizes the need for balance among physical, emotional and social health		

Teacher Comments

Indicators

- Identifies what types of physical activities he/she does and how, when and where they are done.
- Describes positive and negative feelings towards these physical activities.

The Lesson

Discussion points:

- What is your favorite (physical) activity? Why?
- What is an activity you don't like to do? Why?
- With whom do you do these activities?
- What activities do you do by yourself?
- Where do you do them? (School yard, track, park, backyard, etc.)

What to do:

- Depending on the time of year this activity is done, students' answers may need to be dictated or the students may need some other form of assistance. The activity could also be completed orally or with the teacher writing brief answers on a class chart.
- Use the discussion points to develop an understanding of the activity with the students. Encourage a range of activities—ones they like and dislike.
- Students can draw and label four chosen activities before completing the rest of the retrieval chart.
- In the section "How does it make you feel?" students draw a smile or frown on the faces to express their feelings.

Answers:

Answers will vary

Additional Activities

- Make two class booklets entitled "Activities We Like to Do" and "Activities We Don't Like to Do."
- Keep a class list of physical activities students do at school and home throughout the day. Tally these to find the most popular and discuss the reasons why.

Background Information

Several factors influence people's choice of sports or physical activity. Students of this age may not be involved in organized team sports at school or as a member of a club outside of school. Their physical activities will include kicking or throwing balls around at recess, playing on playground equipment, playing chase, using jump ropes, playing marbles, etc. Physical education classes at school will often involve learning skills such as hitting, throwing and catching.

At home, students may be involved in ballet, gymnastics, or swimming lessons. Family activities may include going to the beach, swimming in a backyard pool, hiking, or bike riding.

Other activities will include walking to school and back, skateboarding, rollerblading, and general play with siblings and friends in the backyard or local park.

Students may enjoy some activities more than others depending on whether they find an activity difficult, if they feel too hot or cold doing an activity, or if an activity takes too long to complete.

Activity	By myself	In a group	With family	When and where?	How does it make you feel?

Indicators

- Identifies independent living skills.
- Expresses feelings about exercise and friendships.
- Identifies aspects about himself/herself which develop self-esteem.

The Lesson

Discussion points:

- What are some things you can do by yourself at home?
- What are some things you can do now that you couldn't do when you were younger?
- When do you feel sad/happy/worried?
- Why do we need to exercise?
- How do you feel before, during and after exercising?
- Why do we need friends?
- How do we make new friends?

What to do:

- Introduce the lesson by singing. "This is the way we brush our hair…" etc., using good health habits.
- Read the opening paragraph with the students.
- Read the heading for the first section and Question 1. Allow the students to complete Question 1 by coloring those activities they can do by themselves. Students may not be allowed to attempt some activities because their parents do not allow them to. Make allowance for this when marking the answers.
- Read the next heading and ask the students to complete Question 2 (a), using activities they like to do and activities they do not like to do. Students should list the qualities of their best friend which they like for 2 (b).
- Repeat for Question 3. Students should list something they are good at and something that they are getting better at and how they achieved both.
- Students complete Question 4 by drawing a picture as directed.

Answers:

Answers will vary

Additional Activities

- Students name or list other independent living skills they have.
- Students compile a list of other skills they would like to learn and write about how they could learn them.
- List and compare forms of exercise. Graph the ten most popular ones.
- List the qualities which make a good friend.
- Students draw their best friend(s) and list their qualities on the front or back of the drawing.
- Discuss feelings and the things that promote these feelings. Discuss ways of dealing with feelings such as anger.

Background Information

As students develop independent living skills, they feel more confident and willing to try new things. It is important that students feel able to express themselves and can communicate effectively. Good mental health is as important as physical health.

As we grow older, we can do more things for ourselves.
We become better at saying what we think and feel.
We become better at looking after ourselves.

Caring for your health and becoming independent

1 Color the things you can do by yourself.

brush my teeth		dress myself		comb or brush my hair
wash myself	tie my shoelaces	set the table		exercise
walk to school		make friends		make my own breakfast

Expressing your feelings

2 (a) When I exercise, I like to _____

_____

but I don't like to _____

(b) I like my friend, _____, because _____

_____

Feeling good about yourself

3 (a) I am good at _____ because

_____

(b) I am getting better at _____

because _____

4 Draw yourself exercising with your friends.

Indicators

- Identifies and illustrates rules appropriate for the classroom and the playground.
- Identifies reasons for having rules.
- Recognizes his/her responsibility to keep himself/herself safe by obeying rules.

The Lesson

Discussion points:

- What are some rules you have to follow at home?
- Who makes the rules at your home?
- Do all homes have the same rules? Why/Why not?
- What would happen if there were no rules?
- When is a good time to make rules for playing a game?
- Why are rules important?
- Should rules be changed? If so, when? (Before, during, or after a game?)

What to do:

- Write the word "rules" on the board and ask the students to explain what rules are.
- Read the sentences at the top of the page with the students.
- Discuss Question 1 with the students and allow them to offer suggestions orally. Some students may need assistance from an adult to write unknown words. Others may simply draw the picture and an adult may write for them.
- Discuss Questions 2 and 3 with the students, then allow them to complete their answers. An adult may write for those who need assistance. Some students may give their answers orally to the teacher while others are writing.

Answers

Answers will vary

Additional Activities

- Discuss rules that adults need to follow for their safety; e.g., road rules.
- Compile and list class rules on a large sheet of cardboard in the room. (Students feel more ownership towards rules if they assist in the making of them. Rules should be kept to a minimum and should include a list of "DOS," not "DON'TS.")
- Brainstorm and list rules for home. Highlight the common ones.
- Discuss games which require rules; e.g., card games. Hold a card or game afternoon when the students have had a good week obeying class rules.

Background Information

Students should be familiar with rules at home and at school. Rules can help us to work in a team such as the family, get along with others, play and work safely, and cope with difficult situations. For rules to be effective, students need to be responsible for obeying them and understand why they have been put in place.

We have rules in the classroom and on the playground.
We need rules to keep us safe.

1 Write one rule for the classroom and one for the playground. Draw a boy or girl obeying each rule.

Classroom	**Playground**

2 Why is it good to have rules for the classroom?

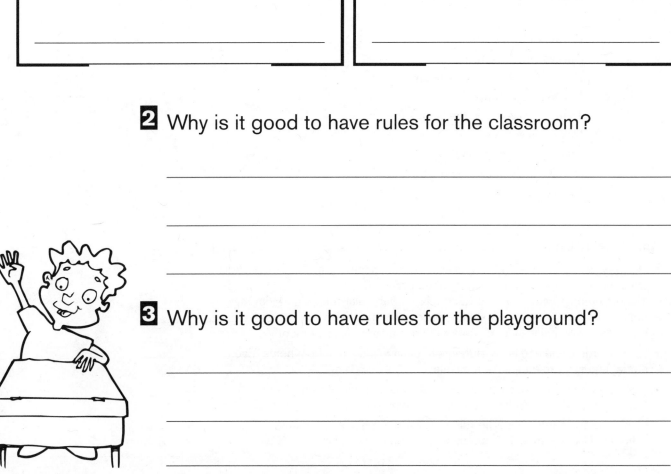

3 Why is it good to have rules for the playground?

Indicators

- Identifies rules appropriate for home.
- Identifies reasons for having rules.
- Recognizes his/her responsibility to keep himself/herself safe by obeying rules.

The Lesson

Discussion points:

- What are some rules you have to follow at home?
- Who makes the rules in your home?
- Do all homes have the same rules? Why/Why not?
- What would happen if there were no rules?
- Why are rules important?
- Should rules be changed? If so, when?

What to do:

- View the picture with the students and discuss which family rules are not being followed.
- Read Question 1 to the students. Explain the instructions. Read each rule and allow the students time to look back at the picture to try to find an example of that rule being disobeyed.
- Discuss why rules are followed at home. Read each statement in Question 2 with the students and allow them to check those statements they think are correct. Discuss answers as a class.

Answers:

1. (a) Put your clothes away.
    (b) Always eat at the table.
    (c) Put your trash in the trash can.
    (d) Put your toys away.
    (e) The dog only sits on the floor.
    (f) Never run in the house.
    (h) Take your shoes off inside.
2. (b) to learn to help each other
    (c) to stay healthy
    (e) to keep ourselves safe

Additional Activities

- Discuss different roles and responsibilities for members of the family and whether or not they like performing these roles. Suggest ways of helping those members who don't like performing a particular role; e.g., Mom may not like to cook dinner every night. A suggestion may be to ask Dad to bring home a cooked chicken for dinner or to have takeout twice a month.
- Form a large circle and allow students to each relate a rule from home. Each student must try to suggest a new rule.
- Survey students (count hands up when a particular rule is mentioned by the teacher) to find out which home rules are common.
- Complete the sentences "The rule I dislike the most is… because…" and "The rule I like the most is… because…" during writing time.

Background Information

Students should be familiar with rules at home and at school. Rules can help us to work in a team such as the family, get along with others, play and work safely, and cope with difficult situations. For rules to be effective, students need to be responsible for obeying them and understand why they have been put in place.

Look at the picture below.

1 Check the boxes for the rules which are not being followed in the picture.

   (a) Put your clothes away. ☐   (b) Always eat at the table. ☐

   (c) Put your trash in the trash can. ☐   (d) Put your toys away. ☐

   (e) The dog only sits on the floor. ☐   (f) Never run in the house. ☐

   (g) Never yell in the house. ☐   (h) Take your shoes off inside. ☐

2 Check the boxes for the correct answers.

We follow rules at home:

(a) because Mom and Dad like to be the "boss." ☐

(b) to learn to help each other. ☐

(c) to stay healthy. ☐

(d) because Mom and Dad are mean. ☐

(e) to keep ourselves safe. ☐

Indicators

- Matches pictures to appropriate rules.
- Writes a rule appropriate to a situation in a picture.

The Lesson

Discussion points:

- What is a rule?
- Why do we need rules?
- What are some rules to use in the classroom?
- What are some rules to use on the playground?
- What are some rules that may be used at home?
- Who makes rules?
- When and how should rules be changed?

What to do:

- Discuss the questions above and record any relevant information on a chart for future use.
- Read the opening paragraph with the students.
- View the pictures in Question 1 and discuss what is happening in each picture.
- Read each rule and ask the students to connect each rule to its matching picture, using a different colored pencil for each one.
- View and discuss the picture in Question 2.
- Students try to think of a rule for the picture such as "Always eat at the table."

Answers:

Answers will vary

Additional Activities

- Remind students of class and playground rules.
- Compare students' home rules to find common ones.
- Discuss "adult" rules, such as those for road safety.
- Discuss games which require rules. Spend one afternoon playing cards or games which require rules to reward the students for obeying class or playground rules.
- If possible, construct class rules at the beginning of the year with the students. Students show more ownership towards a set of rules if they are involved in the compilation of them.
- List characteristics of good team members or good team leadership.

Background Information

Students should be familiar with rules at home and at school. Rules can help us to work in a team such as the family, get along with others, play and work safely, and cope with difficult situations. For rules to be effective, students need to be responsible for obeying them and understand why they have been put in place.

Rules help us to get along with each other. Rules need to be fair and should not change. Rules can help to keep us safe.

1 Match the rules to the pictures.

•   •   Take turns

•   •   Share

•   •   Listen when others are speaking

•   •   Raise your hand to speak

2 Write a rule for this picture.

_____

_____

_____

_____

Indicators

- Identifies activities relevant to a particular age.
- Identifies ways to help at home and at school.

The Lesson

Discussion points:

- What is a "role"?
- What is your role at home?
- Do you have any roles at school?
- Are you responsible for anything at home?
- What are the roles and responsibilities of the members of your family?
- How could you help a family member who has a difficult role to perform?
- How could you help the teacher at school?

What to do:

- Read the first two sentences with the students.
- View the pictures in Question 1. Students identify the age of the person in each picture.
- Students connect those activities relevant to a baby to the picture of the baby, then connect those for an older child to the picture of the older child. Different colored pencils may be used for easy identification.
- Discuss those roles and responsibilities shown in the pictures in Question 2. Students discuss those which they are capable of doing and color only those activities.

Answers:

1. baby: used a pacifier; had a nap during the day; drank from a bottle; had to be carried

    older child: count to 20; ride a bike by myself; write my name; dress myself

2. Teacher check

Additional Activities

- Make a list of responsibilities to be done as a class helper. Students take turns completing each role during the year.
- Reward students who act responsibly in the classroom and on the playground.
- Students select a responsibility to help their parents at home and carry it out. Students report back about likes or dislikes of performing this role and what they have learned.
- Discuss roles students would like to have as grown-ups. This may include occupations, hobbies, or interests to undertake. Ask students to write a story titled "When I Grow Up…"

Background Information

A person's role is his/her expected or usual part in life. People may have many different roles. A responsibility is a duty of care. Within a given role, a person may have certain responsibilities to perform. Roles and responsibilities change with age and environment. Most students are only too willing to perform jobs at home and at school. Children love to help. Giving students roles and responsibilities provides opportunities to learn new skills and develop self-discipline, and provides opportunities for students to enjoy satisfaction and a sense of accomplishment. Responsibility should begin at home with parents giving students age-appropriate tasks to do. People do not always respond in the same way to responsibilities. Less confident people may not wish to take on a leadership role, but may work well within a group, showing that they are still responsible. Other people may act irresponsibly but can still be relied upon. Some people are more responsible in some roles than others.

As you get older, you can do more and help more.
You can do many things that you couldn't do when you were younger.

1 Draw a line from each activity to the correct picture.

ride a bike by myself

count to 20

drank from a bottle

had a nap during the day

When I was younger, I …

Now I am older, I can …

write my name

used a pacifier

had to be carried

dress myself

2 Color and label the ways you can help at home and school now that

Indicators

- Selects right and wrong decisions.
- Illustrates scenarios appropriately.

The Lesson

Discussion points:

- What are some difficult decisions you have had to make?
- What are some easy decisions you have had to make?
- How do you know when a decision is right or wrong?
- How do you feel when you make the right decision?
- How do you feel when you make the wrong decision?
- What can make decisions hard to make? (peer influence)
- Who can you talk to about difficult decisions?

What to do:

- Read and discuss the opening sentences with the students.
- Selected students may read the scenarios to the class or you may read them.
- After each scenario, allow the students time to discuss and color the word yes or no.

Answers:

Answers will vary

Additional Activities

- Relate other scenarios orally to the students and allow them to make the decisions.
- Discuss times when parental permission must be gained before doing something.
- Discuss times when it may be okay to deviate from the rules.
- Read books where characters may need to make decisions.
- List ways of doing the right thing to protect the environment, such as picking up trash, recycling, and conserving water, flora and fauna.
- Students relate news articles which show people or companies doing the right or wrong thing.

Background Information

Children need to learn to think about whether something is right or wrong before making a choice. They need guidelines for making the right decisions, because sometimes deciding on the right choice may not be clear cut. To help children make the right decisions, they may find the following questions helpful to think about before making a decision:

- *Does it feel right? (What does your conscience say?)*
- *Can my decision hurt someone, including myself?*
- *Is it fair?*
- *Would I like it if someone did it to me?*
- *Have I been told not to do this because it is wrong?*
- *How do I really feel about it?*
- *Will I like myself later if I do this?*
- *What would my mom and dad say about it?*

Suggest to children that when a decision proves too difficult, it is a good idea to talk it over with someone they trust and respect.

Every day we have to make decisions.
Some decisions are easy and some are hard.
Deciding to do the right thing can sometimes be difficult.
Sometimes we need to think hard before deciding what
is the right thing to do.

Read each story, then color yes or no to show if the right decision was made.

1 Sam and Todd were playing a computer game. They decided to take turns.

They made the right decision.

| **yes** | **no** |

2 Amanda asked her friend, Sasha, to come to her house after school to play. They walked straight to Amanda's house after school.

They made the right decision.

| **yes** | **no** |

3 Aleisha had to go with her mom to visit her mom's friend, Sarah. Aleisha didn't like Sarah's daughter, so she sulked and was nasty all through the visit.

She made the right decision.

| **yes** | **no** |

4 Kamal and Luke found a Gameboy™ when they were bike riding. They decided to take it home and keep it.

They made the right decision.

| **yes** | **no** |

5 Josh went to Ben's birthday party. There was a lot of food and Josh ate too much. When it was time to eat the birthday cake, Josh asked if he could take his home to eat later.

He made the right decision.

| **yes** | **no** |

Indicators

- Identifies situations where children are cooperating.
- Identifies ways of cooperating.

The Lesson

Discussion points:

- What does it mean to "cooperate"?
- How can you cooperate with others at school and at home?
- When have you seen others cooperating? What were they doing?
- What happens when you don't cooperate?
- Who do you know who cooperates well?
- What are the easiest ways to cooperate?
- What are the hardest ways to cooperate?
- Why do we need to cooperate with each other?

What to do:

- Display a picture of a group of children playing or working together to introduce the topic.
- Discuss the questions above. Refer to children who are cooperating in the picture.
- Ask students to look at picture A in Question 1. As a class, identify situations where students are cooperating with each other. Students circle the situations.
- Repeat the same process with picture B. This picture includes situations where students are not cooperating. Discuss as a class.
- Read the cooperation skills listed in Question 2. Explain any the students don't understand. Explain that (g) means to "compromise" and (h) is talking about showing appreciation to others. Young students are quite happy to learn "big" words, but be sure to ask them to repeat the words.

Answers:

Teacher check

Additional Activities

- Reward students when they display good cooperation skills.
- Read books where people or animals do not cooperate. For example, *The Little Red Hen*.
- Appoint two or more students a group helper's task and expect them to complete this task on a regular basis while working together: for example, handing out equipment or tidying up school work areas.
- Encourage pair or small group discussion work regularly to encourage students to listen to each other.
- Praise and reward students constantly for good work and appropriate behavior.

Background Information

Students need to learn that cooperating with others is a basic life skill that helps them to work successfully with others in groups and to interact with others. Cooperation skills include listening carefully to others to make sure that we fully understand what they are saying; sharing; taking turns; compromising; doing our part in a group activity; showing appreciation to people for what they have done; encouraging people to do their best; making people feel needed; and not isolating or excluding others.

It is important to get along with other people.
This is called "cooperating."

1 Look at the pictures. Circle the children who are cooperating.

2 There are many ways to cooperate. Check the ones that you use.

(a) listen to others ☐

(b) share things ☐

(c) take turns ☐

(d) do my part of a task ☐

(e) encourage others to do their best ☐

(f) make others feel needed ☐

(g) talk about disagreements and decide on a solution ☐

(h) tell others when they have done something good ☐

Indicators

- Identifies actions which show appreciation.
- Follows rules to play a game.

The Lesson

Discussion points:

- Who are the people you interact with each day?
- What are some ways to show someone that you appreciate what they do for you?
- Would you show appreciation in the same way to everyone?
- Would you show appreciation in the same way to the same person each time?
- What are some ways your teacher shows that he/she appreciates good behavior or good work?

What to do:

- The rules of the game are as follows:
  - Players must each have a counter and one die between them.
  - Players take turns to throw the die and count the number of squares to move.
  - When a player lands on an action which shows appreciation, he/she moves forward extra squares.
  - When a player lands on an action which does not show appreciation, he/she goes back.
  - The winner is the player who passes the "Finish" square first.
- You may photocopy enough copies of the game to share between groups of two to four players. Copying onto card stock will make the game more durable.
- Read all the information on the worksheet and allow students to play the game.

Answers:

n/a

Additional Activities

- List easy ways of showing appreciation so students may use them with family, friends and acquaintances.
- Teachers create, and students play, other games which show desirable and undesirable behaviors.
- Praise and reward students constantly for correct behavior.
- Discuss and list nice things to say about other people.
- List jobs to help parents at home and ask students to try to do them occasionally.
- Notice students being good and showing appreciation for others. Award a special merit certificate each week to students "caught being good."

Background Information

Children interact with people every day. They belong to various groups, meet new people, and have close relationships with peers, family and teachers. To develop positive relationships with these people, it is important to show appreciation for them. Appreciation may be shown in various forms such as praise, giving affection and gifts, helping, doing special things, showing consideration, sharing worries and joys, and listening and talking to people. When we show appreciation for other people, we show that they are valued and we enhance relationships.

Start	Say thanks to your mom for making lunch. **Forward 3**		In a hurry. Don't say hello to a buddy. **Back 1**	
				Smile at Mr. Davis, the principal. **Forward 1**
		Share chips from the lunchroom with friends. **Forward 1**	Let a friend go first. **Forward 2**	
Gossip to the new boy and ignore a friend. **Back 1**				
	Say nasty things about another student's work. **Back 3**		Pick a flower on the way home for Mom. **Extra turn**	

The Game
This game is about showing appreciation for others. Each time a player lands on an action showing appreciation for someone, he/she moves forward. But each time a player lands on an action which does not show appreciation for someone, they must go back. This game is suitable for two to four players.

Put bag and shoes away after school. **Forward 1**

		Listen and follow instructions at karate. **Forward 2**		
Hug Dad when he comes home. **Forward 1**				
	Ignore big brother when he complains. **Back 3**		Ignore the dog when he wants to play. **Back 1**	**Finish**

Indicator

- Identifies people and things who/that are special to him/her.

The Lesson

Discussion points:

- What are some of your favorite things?
- Who is special to you?
- Why do we like some things more than others?
- Do we all like the same things? Why/Why not?

What to do:

- Ask students to bring something special to them from home to show and talk about. It could be a toy, ornament, article of clothing, or a photograph of a person or people, pets, or a place.
- Students can take turns sharing their items with the class at show-and-tell sessions or in groups prior to the lesson.
- Discuss the categories of special people and things on the booklet.
- Assist students, if necessary, to cut out and fold the booklet before drawing the pictures.
- Pictures can be labeled if desired.
- Students share their booklet with classmates.

Answers:

Teacher check

Additional Activities

- Students form circles of five or six. A category is given; e.g., the weekend. In turn, students say what is special about the topic.
- Discover what is the same and different about pairs of students. Students draw or write their favorite number, color, fruit, drink, animal, toy, etc. Compare answers.

Background Information

Students will begin to learn about themselves as individuals by identifying what is special in terms of family and friends, their gender, special interests, cultural background and relationships. They describe experiences that give them positive feelings. In doing so, they will learn to realize and value the similarities and differences between themselves and others. This leads into developing respect for the rights, feelings, efforts and achievements of others.

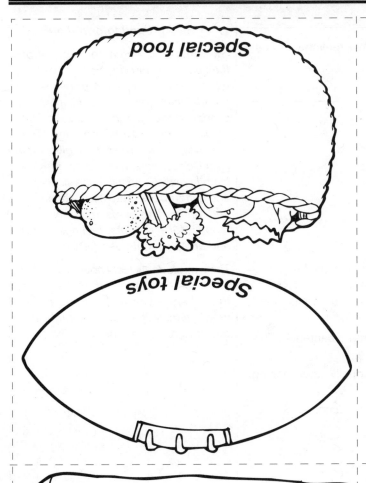

Special food

Special toys

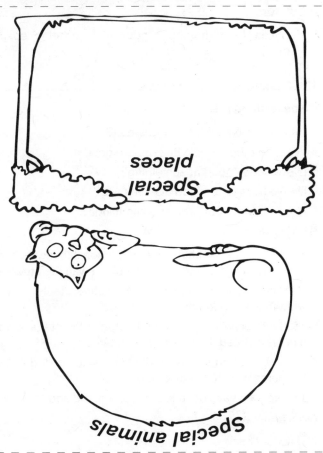

Special places

Special animals

Other things that are special to me ...

My Special Things

My special people

Indicator

- Identifies things he/she is good at to develop positive feelings of self-worth.

The Lesson

Discussion points:

- What do you think you are good at?
- What do other people say you are good at?
- Is everybody good at something?
- Do we have to be good at everything?
- How can you get better at some things?

What to do:

- Students enjoy teachers sharing personal thoughts and feelings. Complete what you do best in the star and share with the students.
- Use the discussion points above to stimulate the students' thoughts about what they are good at.
- Students draw what they are best at in the star and write a sentence. This can be dictated if necessary.
- The second part of the activity can be completed individually, after reading the phrases with the students.
- Two spaces have been left for students to add their own examples.

Answers:

Teacher check

Additional Activities

- Display the completed worksheets for students to view.
- Students make up a four-page booklet similar to that on page 31 about things they are good at.
- Encourage all class members to make positive comments about good things they notice others doing.

Background Information

Students will begin to learn about themselves as individuals by identifying what is special in terms of family and friends, their gender, special interests, academic and sporting abilities, cultural background and relationships. They describe experiences that give them positive feelings. In doing so, they will learn to realize and value the similarities and differences between themselves and others. This leads into developing respect for the rights, feelings, efforts and achievements of others.

The way students feel about themselves has a marked impact on the way they treat themselves and others. If self-worth and self-esteem is high, it is easier to relate to others.

This is what I can do best.

These are other things I am good at ...

being a good friend ☐   making my bed ☐

reading a book ☐   playing games ☐

drawing pictures ☐   listening carefully ☐

helping people ☐   getting dressed ☐

☐   ☐

Indicators

- Reads a poem about individuality.
- Identifies specific aspects which make him/her unique.

The Lesson

Discussion points:

- How are you different from others?
- What are some physical features you have that you like? (Do you have nice eyes, hair, or freckles?)
- What are some things you do well?
- What things do you do well at home?
- What good qualities do you have? (loyal, funny, good leader, good helper, and so on)
- What do people like about you?
- What skills or qualities would you like to have or improve?

What to do:

- Discuss the questions above.
- Read the poem with the students.
- Read the instructions for Question 2. Allow time for students to complete each sentence.
- Students who have written answers may draw a suitable picture in each box if there is enough space.

Answers:

Answers will vary

Additional Activities

- Students write their names and decorate them.
- Students create a poster about themselves using pictures from magazines. Students may cut out any pictures which relate to things they do or like such as favorite foods, hobbies, likes, or favorite colors.
- You may choose a student of the week. This student brings in a photograph of himself/herself and gives a short talk about himself/herself.
- Compare likes and dislikes of the class.
- Hold a special day where students bring in medals, trophies, or awards.
- Ensure that all students have the opportunity to be a class monitor or helper to develop leadership skills.
- Praise, reward and encourage the efforts of all students all the time. Students should be encouraged to "give it a try" as much as possible.

Background Information

Sometimes it is difficult for students to have a clear view of themselves. They exist in a community which expects them to play different roles, many of which involve different behaviors. They are constantly being bombarded with media expectations of body images and materialistic values. They are molded by their own experiences, by culture, sexuality and socioeconomic status, and by peer, familial and gender influences. It is important for a student to be aware that he/she is a multifaceted, unique individual who is valuable.

Identity grows as students relate to different people in different places. Feelings and thoughts are difficult for students to express, but play a valuable part in defining who a person really is and how they respond to others.

It is important to remember that each of us is special.

1 Read the poem "I Am Special."

> *I am special. Can't you see?*
> *You look like you. I look like me.*
> *We don't speak or act or dress alike.*
> *I like to rollerblade. You like your bike.*
>
> *Our families are different. Our feelings aren't the same.*
> *We don't have a lot in common—not even our names.*
> *But I like you and you like me.*
> *Each of us is special—as special as can be!*

2 Write something good about yourself in each box.
Draw a picture for each example.

I like the way I look because ...	At school, I am good at ...

Indicators

- Differentiates between important and unimportant decisions.
- Makes decisions based on positive and negative consequences.

The Lesson

Discussion points:

- How do you know when something you might do is right or wrong?
- Who cares if you do the wrong or right thing?
- Who can you ask to help in making a decision?
- What is an important decision?
- What is a decision that is not important?

What to do:

- Relate the following scenario to the students (or make up your own!).

  You are visiting an ice cream shop with 50 varieties to choose from. What flavor will you choose?

- After discussion, ask students if that was an important decision or not.
- Ask for examples of important decisions.
- Discuss the need for asking someone they trust and respect to help them make certain decisions.
- Explain what the students need to do on the worksheet. Don't discuss answers in detail, as they need to make their own decisions.
- While students are completing the worksheet, assist as required with reading unfamiliar words, dictating text, etc.
- Share answers as a whole class. Discuss why particular decisions were made.

Answers:

Teacher check

Additional Activities

- Discuss the saying "Finders keepers, losers weepers."
- Role-play the scenarios on the worksheet in small groups performed in front of the class.
- List decisions which students can not necessarily make for themselves and discuss who makes them; e.g., what they eat for dinner (Mom or Dad); who they sit next to in class (teacher).

Background Information

Some decisions require making a choice between something that is right or wrong. At this age, an example would be whether or not to use someone's colored pencils without asking. Other decisions are not very important; e.g., Do I eat my ham sandwich first or have a drink of water?

Whatever the decision, young children need to learn to make up their minds and practice making decisions for themselves. They need to look at the consequences of making a particular decision and learn to live with it if it is wrong. Children may need to talk about a possible decision with someone they trust and respect.

1 Sometimes it can be hard deciding what to do.
Draw or write about what decision you would make for each of these.

(a) Who will you play with at recess tomorrow?

(b) What will you wear to school tomorrow?

(c) Who will you invite to your next birthday party?

(d) What would you do if you found a $10 bill?

2 Should you wash your hands before eating? | yes | no |

Why? _____

_____

3 A stranger starts talking to you. What things would you do?

tell an adult	walk or run away	talk to him/her	giggle	don't talk to him/her

Indicators

- Identifies people who make specific decisions.
- Retells a good and a bad decision.

The Lesson

Discussion points:

- Why do adults make a lot of decisions for children?
- Do you agree with these decisions? Why/Why not?
- What decisions made by adults would you like to make for yourself?
- How do you know when you have made the right decision? How do you feel?
- How do you feel when you know you have made the wrong decision?
- What are "consequences"?
- Does knowing possible consequences help you to decide what to do?
- What are some good and bad consequences of decision making in different situations?
- What are some steps to make decision making easier?

What to do:

- Discuss the questions above.
- Read the opening sentences and the instructions for Question 1.
- Read each decision with the students and allow them time to check the relevant box. NOTE: Some decisions may be made by more than one person. For example, "The books I read" may be decided by the teacher at school, the student at the library and a parent at bedtime.
- Explain what "bad" and "good" decisions are.
- Read Question 2. Students write about a decision they made that was bad or had bad consequences.
- Repeat for Question 3.

Answers:

Answers will vary

Additional Activities

- Within guidelines, allow students to make age-appropriate decisions at school as much as possible.
- Relate scenarios where decisions have to be made and allow students to discuss choices.
- Discuss situations that arise in the class or playground that require choices to be made. Decide whether decisions are good or bad.
- List the qualities of a good decision maker.
- Allow students to view the decision-making steps on a chart.
- Discuss other people or things that may influence decisions. For example, friends, background, etc.
- Discuss the possibility that even when a bad decision has been made, students will learn from their experiences.

Background Information

It is important students learn to stop and think about whether something is right or wrong before making a choice.

Having choices and making decisions can have consequences, both positive and negative. Students need to become independent and in control of some of the aspects of their life, and learn to face the consequences.

The steps for decision making are:

1. Define the problem.

2. Brainstorm possible solutions.

3. Evaluate the ideas and consider all consequences.

4. Decide on a solution and carry it out.

People have to make decisions every day.
Some decisions are small and some are very important.
Sometimes other people need to make decisions for you.

1 Check the boxes to show who makes these decisions for you.

Decision	Me	Parent	Friend	Teacher	Other
What I have for breakfast	☐	☐	☐	☐	☐
The books I read	☐	☐	☐	☐	☐
My hairstyle for the day	☐	☐	☐	☐	☐
The games I play at school	☐	☐	☐	☐	☐
The clothes I wear	☐	☐	☐	☐	☐
Who I play with	☐	☐	☐	☐	☐
Who I sit next to in class	☐	☐	☐	☐	☐
What I eat for dinner	☐	☐	☐	☐	☐
When I do my homework	☐	☐	☐	☐	☐
What I watch on TV	☐	☐	☐	☐	☐

2 Write about a "bad" decision you made by yourself.

_____

_____

3 Write about a "good" decision you made by yourself.

_____

_____

Indicators

- Recognizes situations that make him/her angry.
- Identifies ways to deal with anger.

The Lesson

Discussion points:

- Talk about situations that make the students feel angry.
- Discuss how they feel and what they do when they are angry (cry, yell, etc.).
- Is it okay to get angry sometimes? When?
- What could you do if you feel yourself getting angry?

What to do:

- Explain a scenario of a situation involving anger to students (hand or finger puppets could be used for characters). Suggestions: someone knocking over a tower of blocks, someone teasing someone else about his/her haircut or clothes, or someone pushing someone else over in the sandbox.
- Ask students to talk about times when they felt angry.
- Discuss how they felt, what they looked like and how they acted.
- Discuss the actions and feelings that are acceptable and those that are not.
- Ask what could be done to help control anger.
- Students complete Question 1 and share with a partner.
- Read each of the actions in Question 2. Students can decide individually whether to color with red or yellow.
- Compare answers as a class.

Answers:

Teacher check

Additional Activities

- Students can role-play what they have drawn and written about in Question 1.
- Display a chart of suggestions to follow if they feel anger building up too much. Base the text on the background information.
- Use picture stories and cartoon strips from magazines to discuss how characters deal with anger, particularly in positive ways.

Background Information

An important self-management skill is learning self-control. Students need to use self-control (the ability to stop themselves from doing something) to deal with anger, in particular, and also to prevent themselves from becoming overexcited.

Unacceptable ways of expressing anger include hitting and pushing, sulking and crying excessively, or constantly looking for comfort solutions from a teacher or adult. Suggested steps for anger management or helping to gain control of emotions include:

1. *Stop and take a deep breath, or walk away.*

2. *Think and choose the best way to act.*

3. *Stay calm and in control.*

4. *Talk about feelings.*

What makes you feel angry?

1 Draw and write about something that made you angry.

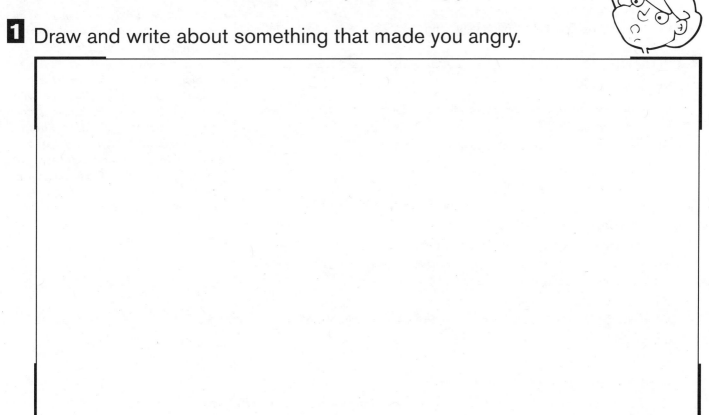

What do you do when you are angry?

2 Color the good things to do in yellow.
Color the bad things to do in red.

yell and shout	hit someone	walk away
count to 10		cry all the time
kick something		talk to someone
take a deep breath		think about what to do

Indicators

- Identifies strengths and weaknesses.
- Relates feelings about attempting new things.

The Lesson

Discussion points:

- What are some things you can do now that you couldn't do last year or when you were a toddler?
- What are some things you are good at?
- What are some things you are not good at?
- Are we all good at the same things?
- Do you always enjoy doing the things you are good at? Why/Why not?
- Do you always hate doing things you are not good at? Why/Why not?
- How do you feel when you have to try something new?
- How do you feel when you try something new and you do well? How about when you do not do as well as you hoped?
- Why is it good to fail sometimes?
- What should you do if you fail many times trying a particular thing?

What to do:

- Discuss the questions above.
- Read the opening sentences and the instructions for Question 1.
- Read each activity with the students and allow them time to circle or cross through it.
- Read Question 2 and allow students time to answer.
- Repeat for Question 3.
- Students complete the page by drawing a picture for Question 4.

Answers:

Answers will vary

Additional Activities

- Reward and praise students constantly for trying, whether they succeed or not.
- Encourage risk-taking attempts when reading and writing stories.
- Ensure the classroom climate is such that students feel comfortable to try new things and know that they are allowed to fail sometimes.
- Name and list some well-known people who have excelled in their chosen field.
- Discuss people with disabilities who have succeeded where "able" people may have failed.
- Display trophies, awards, medals and certificates students may bring in.
- Choose one person each week as "Best Achiever" (i.e., the student who tries hard to achieve something they are not good at—whether they succeed or not!).
- Provide opportunities for students to acknowledge their mistakes and think about how to rectify them. This is a valuable learning experience for students.
- Reward students for showing appreciation and encouraging others.

Background Information

As unique, valuable individuals, we all have our strengths and weaknesses. It is important to be pleased with our successes as well as the way in which we handle failure. This can be as difficult for adults to cope with as it is for children. Risk taking can be very hard and children should be praised and rewarded for any attempts to try something new, not just their successes. Quite often it is necessary to attempt a new thing many times before succeeding. In this way, valuable knowledge, skills and values will be learned.

Each of us is good at some things and not so good at others.

1 Look at the activities below.
Circle those you are good at and cross out those you are not so good at.

> ***tying shoelaces***   *drawing*   making the bed
> writing stories
> speaking in front   **handwriting**
> of people   **running**   ***playing***
> ***soccer***
> doing handstands   ***reading***
> making new friends   swimming   **riding a bike**

2 (a) Write something else you are
good at.

(b) Write something else you are
not very good at.

_____

_____

3 (a) How do you feel when you have to try something new?

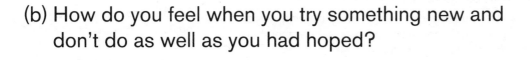

_____

(b) How do you feel when you try something new and
don't do as well as you had hoped?

_____

(c) How do you feel when you try something new and do well?

_____

4 Draw a picture of you doing something you are really good at.

Indicator

- Identifies bullying situations in a variety of scenarios.

The Lesson

Discussion points:

- Sometimes it is difficult to work out if an action is bullying or not. Students must differentiate between a friendly tease as opposed to an intentionally upsetting remark that continues.
  - Would you like it to happen to you?
  - Is what is happening hurting the person's feelings?
  - Is the person being hurt?
  - Is the person afraid?
  - What do people who bully look like? Are they boys, girls, or both? Are they tall or short?

What to do:

- Enlarge one copy of the worksheet so students can view it on a bulletin board. Ask the students what they think each picture shows.
- Work through the discussion points to assist in deciding which situations involve bullying and which do not.
- Students color and complete their own worksheet with personal choices based on the discussion.

Answers:

Teacher check

Additional Activities

- Compile a list of words with the students that describe a person who bullies and a person who does not bully. For example, mean, unkind, nasty, punches, calls you names; friendly, hugs you, smiles, shares toys.
- Discuss other situations where students decide if each is bullying or not. Situations in the classroom or playground from class or school members could be used, but actual names should not be given.

Background Information

Most definitions of bullying agree:

- *it is deliberately hurtful (physically and psychologically).*
- *it is repeated often over time.*
- *it is difficult for the person being bullied to defend himself/herself against it—he/she is weaker physically or psychologically.*

Bullying can be divided into three types:

1. *Physical—hitting, punching, pinching, tripping, spitting, kicking, pushing, scratching, and damaging, hiding, or taking belongings.*

2. *Verbal—name-calling, making offensive remarks, insulting someone.*

3. *Emotional—spreading rumors/ nasty stories about someone, making fun of someone, excluding from groups, ignoring, ostracizing, alienating.*

Children (or adults) who bully others can come from any kind of family, regardless of social class or cultural background.

People who bully vary in their physical appearance, as do the people they bully. It is actions which identify a person who bullies.

Look at the pictures below.
Circle yes if it could be bullying.
Circle no if it is not bullying.

Indicators

- Identifies bullying situations.
- Identifies strategies to cope with bullying situations.

The Lesson

Discussion points:

- What happens when you are bullied?
- What are some ways people can be bullied?
- Do some types of bullying hurt more than others? Explain.
- Which types of bullying are easier to cope with?
- Which types of bullying are more difficult to cope with?
- What can you do if you are being bullied?
- Who can you go to for help if you are being bullied?
- Why do you think people bully other people?

What to do:

- Discuss the questions above.
- Read the opening sentences and the instructions.
- Discuss what is happening in each picture and how each situation might be resolved. Students may suggest several solutions. If possible, encourage students to choose a solution that involves each person dealing with the situation himself/herself.
- Briefly write words or a sentence on the board to reflect the students' answers. Students may copy or write the solutions they feel are suitable.
- Students may color the pictures while others are finishing. You may take this time to ask specific students why they chose a particular solution.

Answers:

Answers will vary

Additional Activities

- Encourage students to relate situations where they may have been bullied and ask them to say how they dealt with them. Do not force students to tell any information which may be distressing or embarrassing for them.
- Create a network picture to show people students trust to go to when they have problems.
- Practice problem-solving skills.
- Encourage students to be assertive. Practice being confident; i.e., using correct body language, maintaining eye contact and speaking clearly.
- Encourage tolerance so that fewer bullying situations occur. Do this by appreciating each others' similarities and differences.
- Be consistent and fair to all students. Do not play favorites.
- Provide a happy, secure and safe environment where students are able to express their feelings and know that they will be listened to when they find themselves being bullied.

Background Information

Bullying is very common within our schools. Students bully for many reasons, including not fitting in, disliking themselves, peer pressure, wanting to show off, feeling upset or angry, and having a fear of being bullied themselves.

Bullying takes many forms, including physical abuse such as hitting, punching and tripping; verbal abuse such as name-calling, teasing and put-downs; and emotional abuse such as gossiping, spreading rumors or making fun of someone, using threatening looks or gestures, and excluding or ignoring someone.

Students should be able to recognize bullying situations. They should be shown appropriate strategies to cope with bullying and be encouraged to use them.

Some strategies include problem-solving, role-play, tolerance, communication, conflict resolution, avoidance, learning when to ask for help and being assertive (not aggressive).

People who bully pick on people smaller or weaker than themselves.
They can make you feel worried, sad and angry if they do not leave you alone.

All the children in the pictures are being bullied.
How do you think they should deal with what is happening?

Indicators

- Identifies with the feelings of someone being bullied.
- Understands strategies to use if he/she is bullied.

The Lesson

Discussion points:

- How does someone being bullied feel?
- How does someone who bullies feel?
- What could you do if you were being bullied?
- Should you tell tales to the teacher?
- When is it okay to tell tales?
- Why do you think people bully?

What to do:

- Students color the two pictures in Question 1 showing bullying situations, and can talk about them and listen to you and others discuss the situations. Use some of the discussion points to ask students and encourage them to ask their own questions.
- Students can complete Question 2 individually. Ask students to read each word or tell them what the words are if no one can read them.
- Follow the same procedure for Question 3, but discuss what each suggestion means before students check or cross through each box.

Answers:

Teacher check

Additional Activities

- Students draw and label pictures of special people they trust who they could ask for help.
- List situations when it is okay to tell the teacher about something and when it is not.
- Read the story *The Boy who Cried Wolf* to reinforce the importance of telling the truth.

Background Information

People who bully do so for many reasons.

A summary of reasons includes:

- *They may feel upset or angry or feel they don't fit in.*
- *They want to appear tough and show off.*
- *They may get bullied themselves by family members.*
- *They're scared of getting picked on, so do it first.*
- *If they don't like themselves, they may take it out on someone else.*
- *They think they will become more popular.*

It is imperative students realize that bullying is not to be tolerated and they should not put up with it if it is happening to them. Keeping it a secret from adults they trust gives the bullies more power to continue.

These are some things the students should not do.

1. *Try to keep dealing with the problem themselves—it is all right to ask for help.*

2. *Exaggerate or not tell the true facts. If a part of what they say is shown to be untrue, it casts doubt upon the whole situation.*

3. *Don't retaliate by hitting, etc. They could end up being accused of bullying themselves.*

---

1 Look at the pictures below.

2 Color the words that describe how you think the children being bullied feel.

| sad | | worried | | angry |

| scared | | | | sick |

| happy | | | | friendly |

3 Check the good things to do if you are bullied.
Cross through the things you should not do.

ignore him/her

say you don't like it

fight with him/her

go to a safe place

tell a teacher or adult

let him/her have his/her own way

don't tell anyone

Indicators

- Identifies qualities which maintain good relationships.
- Completes a crossword about maintaining friendships.

The Lesson

Discussion points:

- Who is your best friend?
- Why is this person your best friend?
- Are all your friends school friends?
- Are you friends with the same people you were friends with last year?
- What makes a good friend?
- Are you a good friend?
- If so, why are you a good friend?
- If not, how can you become a good friend?

What to do:

- Discuss the questions above and the opening paragraph.
- Read through the clues with the students.
- Students complete the crossword, circling each word as it is used.

Answers:

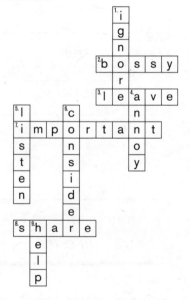

Additional activities

- Create a "My Best Friend" art gallery. Students paint a portrait of their best friend and display it in the room.
- Students write a description of their best friend.
- List qualities needed to be a good friend.
- Discuss the concept of pets as best friends. Talk about why they are good friends and how to show them that they are appreciated.
- Discuss steps for making a new friend, such as how to start conversations with new students at school.
- Hold a "new friend hour" where students spend time in class getting to know and playing with a person they don't usually play with. Allocate partners to students to ensure that no student is left isolated.

Everyone likes to have friends. Friends are fun to be with.
It is good to share things with friends at home and at school.
It is not always easy to be a good friend.

Complete the crossword below to find ways to be a good friend.
Use the words in the box. Circle each word as you use it.

| share important leave bossy help consider listen annoy ignore |

Across

2. I try not to be _____ when we play games.

3. I don't _____ my friends out when I do something.

7. I make my friends feel _____.

8. I can _____ my worries with my friends.

Down

1. I don't _____ my friends and play with other children.

4. I try not to _____ my friends with my bad habits.

5. I talk and _____ to my friends.

6. I _____ my friends' feelings.

9. I try to _____ my friends if they need me.

Indicators

- Identifies family members and how he/she is cared for by them.
- Identifies other people who care for them.

The Lesson

Discussion points:

- Who are the people in your family?
- Are all families the same?
- How do families differ?
- How do the members of your family care for each other?
- How do you help each other at home?
- Who is your favorite family member? Why/Why not?
- Are pets part of the family? Why?
- Who are other people who care for you?

What to do:

- Introduce the topic with a rhyme or song about families.
- Discuss the questions above.
- Read Question 1 with the students. Students draw each family member inside a section of the circle and write each name. An adult may need to write the words for some students. Students may write words such as "cook dinner," "takes me to soccer," etc., next to each picture inside or outside the circle. Family members who do the same caring task may be joined to that word with a pencil line.
- Discuss other people who provide care and list some names on the board. These may include grandparents, babysitters, coaches, day care workers, doctors, or dentists. Students complete Question 2.

Answers:

Teacher check

Additional Activities

- Group students by the number of family members, children, boys, or girls in the family, etc.
- Read stories about families helping each other.
- Write a story about "My Family."
- Paint a family portrait.
- Construct a home for a family and make cylinder "people" to put in the house.

Background Information

Every day, children interact with a variety of people—parents, friends, teachers, relatives and day care workers. Children react to each of these people differently. Relationships with other people are very important, because they give us a sense of who we are and where we belong. They give us comfort and support. Relationships may change or develop over time as children grow older and more independent. Children need to develop skills to maintain happy, healthy relationships. These skills include communication, changing bad habits, negotiation, self-respect and love.

Families care for each other.

1 In the shape below, draw pictures of the members of your family and write each name. Draw yourself in the middle. Next to each person, write a word or words to tell how each person cares for you.

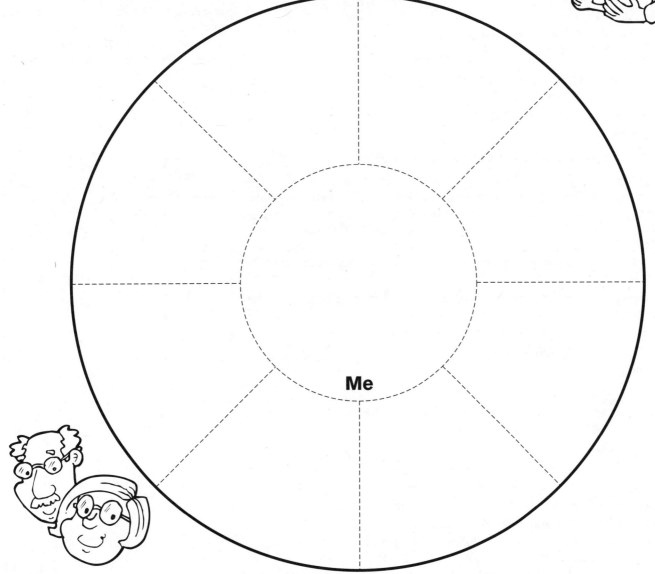

2 Sometimes other people care for us too. Write their names below.

_____

_____

_____

Indicators

- Identifies skills used for getting along with other people.
- Identifies that not all interpersonal skills are used for all people.

The Lesson

Discussion points:

- Who are the people you interact with every day?
- Do you get along with all of them?
- If not, then why not?
- How can we get along with other people?
- What skills do we need to get along with people better?
- Why are some people easier to get along with than others?
- When we get along with others, how do we feel?
- How do others feel when we try to get along with them better?

What to do:

- Introduce the topic with a rhyme or song about friends.
- Discuss the questions above.
- Read the first sentence with the students. Read each skill with the students, and then the name of the person. Ask them to draw a check in the column if they use the skill to get along with that person. Continue in this way until all the skills have been done. Students are not expected to draw a check in each box for every person. Some skills may be easier to use with particular people.
- Students select a person of their own choosing, such as a coach, and the teacher reads each skill again until the final column is completed.
- Students draw a picture of their chosen person.
- Work may be collected for interesting background information about each student.

Answers:

Teacher check

Additional Activities

- If desired, students may count the checks in each column to see which skill they use more than others with particular people.
- Read stories or rhymes about people or animals getting along with each other (or not getting along with each other).
- Practice listening to each other. Students pair up and one person talks for one minute about a given topic while the other student listens. At the end of the time period, the student who was listening retells the information while the first student indicates if he/she was listening or not.
- Try to find one nice thing to say to a different person each day.
- Give each student the responsibility of being a class helper for a day.
- Praise and reward students constantly for good work and appropriate behavior.

Background Information

Every day, children interact with a variety of people—parents, friends, teachers, relatives and day care workers. Children react to each of these people differently. Relationships with other people are very important, because they give us a sense of who we are and where we belong. They give us comfort and support. Relationships may change or develop over time as children grow older and more independent. Children need to develop skills to maintain happy, healthy relationships. These skills include communication, changing bad habits, negotiation, self-respect and love.

We need to learn to get along with the people we see every day.
Getting along with other people makes everyone happy.

Draw a check in the column if you use that skill to get along with each person. The last column has been left for you to choose another person.

Skill	A family member	My best friend	My teacher	
I talk to him/her.				
I listen to him/her.				
I try not to annoy him/her.				
I try not to be bossy.				
I consider his/her feelings.				
I make him/her feel important.				
I try to help him/her.				
I can say what I think.				
I can share my worries.				
I don't leave out or ignore him/her.				

Indicators

- Identifies actions which show love and respect.
- Matches actions to specific people.

The Lesson

Discussion points:

- Who are the people you love and respect?
- What things can we do to show these people we love and respect them?
- What are some things you have done to show someone you love and respect him/her?
- How would you like your family and friends to show you that they love you?
- What is the nicest thing you have done for someone to show him/her you love and respect him/her?

What to do:

- Introduce the activity with a song or rhyme about family and friends.
- Discuss the questions above.
- Carefully view the pictures and make sure the students are aware of who each picture represents.
- Students connect the person/pet to the action that is most appropriate. NOTE: Some actions may be appropriate for more than one person, but for this purpose only one action fits each person.
- Read Question 2. Students can answer in their own words.

Answers:

1. Mom – help by bringing in the washing
    Dad – pass him the tools he needs
    Friend – invite her to my house to play
    Dog – take him for a walk
    Coach – listen to and follow training instructions
    Grandma – let her cuddle me even though I'm big
    Teacher – always put up my hand to speak
    Brother – be quiet while he does his homework
    Sister – ask before I borrow her things
    Grandpa – help him out of the lounge chair
2. Teacher check

Additional Activities

- Students relate other actions they have used to show love and respect to their grandparents, teachers, coaches, siblings and pets.
- Students think of one nice thing to do each day to show love and respect to others. Relate these to the class to give others ideas.
- "Catch" a student being nice each day and reward him/her appropriately.
- Students keep a record of good deeds in an individual booklet and are rewarded at the end of a certain time frame. Students may only enter a deed with teacher approval.

Background Information

Every day, children interact with a variety of people—parents, friends, teachers, relatives and day care workers. Children react to each of these people differently. Relationships with other people are very important, because they give us a sense of who we are and where we belong. They give us comfort and support. Relationships may change or develop over time as children grow older and more independent. Children need to develop skills to maintain happy, healthy relationships. These skills include communication, changing bad habits, negotiation, self-respect and love.

It is important to show our family and friends that we care about them.
There are many ways to do this.

1 Match the action to the person or pet it is best suited for.

- invite her to my house to play

- ask before I borrow her things

- make her a cup of tea

- help him rake up the leaves

- be quiet while he does his homework

- help him out of the lounge chair

- always put up my hand to speak

- let her cuddle me even though I'm big

- take him for a walk

- listen to and follow training instructions

2 Think of the nicest thing you have done for someone.
Write about it below.

_____

_____

_____

Indicator

• Identifies feelings experienced in particular situations.

The Lesson

Discussion points:

• List situations where students feel a particular emotion.

• Which situations do students feel the same about?

• Which situations do students have different feelings about?

• Which feelings are good? (positive)

• Which feelings are bad? (negative)

What to do:

• Brainstorm "feeling" words with the students. Have them (and yourself) express each emotion. Students could work face to face in pairs for this activity.

• List the words on the board or chart and draw a face (if possible) next to each to help students identify them. They will need to refer to them for the worksheet activity. Include happy, sad, excited, angry, worried, nervous, surprised, scared, shy, etc.

• Students complete Question 1 by matching each face to a word. Read the words if necessary.

• Students can refer to the list of feeling words to assist in answering Question 2. Read through each statement with the students or ask a volunteer to read them. Allow time for them to draw a face or copy or write a word from the chart.

• Share responses as a whole class and compare answers.

Answers:

1. Teacher check
2. Answers will vary

Additional Activities

• Practice using facial expressions, stance and body position to show anger, sadness, shyness, happiness, excitement, worry, etc., in order to learn to read others' feelings.

• View and discuss facial expressions of characters in shared reading books.

Background Information

Body language, such as facial expression, stance and position, is key in knowing how a person is feeling. Different situations evoke different emotions. Students should be aware that each of us may react to different situations in different ways. Other situations may evoke similar emotions, such as excitement about a birthday party.

Students need to learn to show feelings in ways that are helpful to them and others and not in ways that are hurtful.

---

1 Look at these faces. They show different feelings.
Match each face to a word.

excited   sad   scared   angry   worried

2 Draw a face or write about how you would feel.

(a)	You are going to the zoo on Saturday.	(b)	You are left out of a game.
(c)	Someone hit you.	(d)	You got all your spelling words right.
(e)	It rained all day.	(f)	You fell off your bike.
(g)	You went to a new school.	(h)	You got lost in a crowd.
(i)	Your best friend is sick.	(j)	You dropped your dinner plate.

Indicators

- Identifies feelings for a given situation.
- Identifies situations which evoke particular feelings.

The Lesson

Discussion points:

- When do you feel happy, sad, angry, excited, worried, or frightened?
- Can you feel more than one emotion in a particular situation?
- Does everyone feel the same in the same situation? Why/Why not?
- How do you cope when you get angry? What do you do?
- Can other people help you when you are feeling sad, angry, or worried?
- Who are the people who help you?
- How do you feel when someone hurts your feelings?
- Have you ever hurt anyone else's feelings?
- How can you fix a situation when you have hurt someone else's feelings?

What to do:

- Introduce the activity with a song or rhyme about feelings, such as "If You're Happy and You Know It, Clap Your Hands."
- Discuss the questions above.
- Read each example in Question 1 with the students and allow them time to write about how it would make them feel.
- Read each part of Question 2, ensuring that students are aware of the feeling represented by each face. Allow them time to complete each example.

Answers:

Answers will vary

Additional activities

- Compare feelings shown in the same situation.
- Create a series of "I feel…" books. Students write a story and illustrate a page for each book about anger, sadness, happiness, excitement, worry, etc. Keep in the class library and encourage students to read them during free time.
- Role-play different emotions using facial expressions and body language.
- Discuss the feelings experienced by particular characters in books.
- Devise simple strategies for dealing with anger management.
- Discuss ways of saying how you feel without hurting anyone else's feelings.

Background Information

Different situations evoke different emotions for different people. People's reactions are influenced by their personalities and backgrounds. Students should feel confident to express their feelings in family and school situations. Classrooms should be comfortable and secure places for students. Teachers should be open-minded and approachable.

At times, students may experience a number of different feelings relating to one particular situation. For example, a new baby coming into the family may evoke feelings of excitement, worry about changing family dynamics, and anger at being replaced as the "baby of the family." Students should be aware that all these reactions are perfectly natural and there is no need to be ashamed of them. The important thing is learning to deal with them in a positive way.

We can have many different feelings.

1 Read each sentence and write how it would make you feel.

(a)   Mom and Dad take me to the zoo.   I feel _____.

(b)   My little brother crushes my model plane.   I feel _____.

(c)   Dad has to go away for a long time for work. I feel _____.

(d)   Mom is having a baby.   I feel _____.

(e)   My birthday party is coming closer.   I feel _____.

(f)   We are moving to a new neighborhood.   I feel _____.

We can say how we feel.

2 (a)   I feel angry when _____

_____

_____

(b)   I feel happy when _____

_____

_____

(c)   I feel excited when _____

_____

_____

Indicator

- Identifies ways of cooperating and communicating effectively.

The Lesson

Discussion points:

- What are some things you should do to be a good listener?
- Why is it important to speak clearly?
- How can you be a good group member?
- Introduce the word "cooperate." Brainstorm words to describe a cooperative person.

What to do:

- The illustration on page 53 can be used in a variety of ways to incorporate listening, speaking and cooperative skills.

    1. Students listen carefully to the teacher, who gives directions one by one to color and add items to the picture. Suggestions are:
        - Color the dog brown and white.
        - Draw a hat on the girl who is patting the cat.
        - Draw a blue bucket on the pier.
        - Draw a seagull flying over the jet ski.

        Read each instruction only once. Speak slowly and clearly and allow time for students to complete each instruction.

    2. Students can make up their own directions for a partner or small group to carefully listen to and follow. The student must speak clearly, slowly and concisely to enable others to understand what to do.

    3. Students can cooperate in pairs or in a small group and decide on how to color the picture and what to add to the picture. You can observe how well each pair or group is cooperating and intervene when necessary to give praise, encouragement, or suggestions as to how the pair or group could work better together.

Answers:

Answers will vary

Additional Activities

- Games such as "Pass the Message," and "My Grandmother went to the Market" are useful in developing listening skills.
- Students describe experiences when they feel uncooperative and explain or determine why (lack of sleep, feeling unwell, something has upset them).
- In pairs or groups, take part in activities such as completing jigsaw puzzles, constructing a building out of blocks or recycled materials, tidying an area, or taking part in a cooking activity.

Background Information

Appropriate communication skills and cooperative behaviors when interacting with others are vital to developing interpersonal relationships. Verbal and non-verbal methods of communication include facial expressions, body language, tone, volume, and clarity of voice.

Other cooperative behaviors besides listening skills include taking turns, sharing, inviting others to join in, showing appreciation and encouraging others.

Many people fail to correctly interpret what other people are saying for a number of reasons. They may be preparing their own responses, the speaker may not have the attention of the audience so their focus may wander to other things, or those listening may feel the need to say something and therefore interrupt rather than letting the other person finish first.

Listening is a skill vital in all areas of learning. It may be learned and developed in a number of ways. Listening to audio tapes and stories, following directions, listening to instructions and repeating messages are some activities which help to develop communication skills.

How to be a good listener

- *Look at the speaker.*
- *Listen without interrupting (or fidgeting).*
- *Concentrate on what the speaker is saying.*
- *Ask questions to find out more.*
- *Show understanding by nodding, etc.*
- *Repeat what you have heard in your own words.*

Indicators

- Completes an acrostic about sharing.
- Completes a word search using "negotiation" words.

The Lesson

Discussion points:

- Why do we need to share?
- Is it easy to share? Why/Why not?
- Can we learn to share? How can we do this?
- What does "negotiate" mean?
- Why is listening important when negotiating?
- How can we make sure that both parties "win" when negotiating?
- What does "compromise" mean?
- Is it necessary to compromise to negotiate?

What to do:

- Introduce the activity with a math activity that involves sharing counters, candy, or toys. Ask the students why it is better to share than to not.
- Discuss the questions above.
- Read the opening sentences and the acrostic to the students, leaving out the unknown words.
- Read the words at the side which need to go in the acrostic.
- Read the acrostic again, allowing the students to choose and write the missing words from the list. Students should cross out each word as they use it. Repeat until the acrostic is finished. Read the completed acrostic together.
- In Question 2, the words in bold can be found in the word search. Students draw a line through each word as it is found.

Answers:

1. better, friends, same, Important, all, practice

2.

s	m	f	b	u	x	s	z	v	s	w
j	b	c	r	i	b	g	c	g	i	c
c	s	h	a	k	e	j	s	n	d	s
i	l	j	l	g	s	g	b	s	g	j
s	i	c	n	b	j	s	g	c	i	r
b	s	g	s	o	l	u	t	i	o	n
c	t	a	t	g	s	r	b	d	r	a
n	e	g	o	t	i	a	t	e	i	c
g	h	r	r	a	s	c	b	c	s	c
j	g	e	m	l	j	c	s	i	r	e
c	b	e	s	k	s	e	b	d	j	p
s	r	j	p	s	e	p	c	e	r	t

Additional Activities

- Participate in math activities and games where sharing is needed.
- Display the negotiation steps in the room for the students to see constantly.
- Reward students who share during break times and in the classroom.
- Practice the negotiating steps in the classroom and encourage students to try them in the playground.

Background Information

It is important for students to be able to share with each other. Sometimes this can be difficult since the world of most children centers around themselves and their own small section of the world.

Learning to share and negotiate are very important skills to learn. Pre-negotiation skills may be taught from school entry. These include skills for positive social behaviors and relationships such as:

- *self-esteem.*
- *awareness of own and others' feelings.*
- *empathy (respecting diversity and differences in others).*
- *anger management/self-control.*
- *communication.*
- *listening.*
- *searching for solutions (problem-solving).*
- *taking responsibility for own actions.*

The negotiation steps are shown on the student worksheet.

It can be hard to share at times. We want to make sure we don't miss out and that we get our fair share. Sometimes we are upset or angry with people and don't feel like sharing.

1 Complete the acrostic by filling in the missing words.

Sharing

Helps us to get along _____ with our _____

And makes sure that everyone is treated the _____.

Really good "sharers" make sure that no one feels more

I_____ than anyone else.

No-one shares well _____ the time but it

Gets easier if you _____.

| |
| all |
| practice |
| friends |
| same |
| Important |
| better |

2 Look at the word search to find some skills to help you to negotiate well.

s	m	f	b	u	x	s	z	v	s	w
j	b	c	r	i	b	g	c	g	i	c
c	s	h	a	k	e	j	s	n	d	s
i	l	j	i	g	s	g	b	s	g	j
s	i	c	n	b	j	s	g	c	i	r
b	s	g	s	o	l	u	t	i	o	n
c	t	a	t	g	s	r	b	d	r	a
n	e	g	o	t	i	a	t	e	i	c
g	n	r	r	a	s	c	b	c	s	c
j	g	e	m	l	j	c	s	i	r	e
c	b	e	s	k	s	e	b	d	j	p
s	r	j	p	s	e	p	c	e	r	t

The steps to **negotiate** are:

• I **talk** about what happened, what I feel and what I want.

• I **listen** to the other person do the same. I don't interrupt!

• We **brainstorm** solutions to suit us both.

• We **decide** on the best solution.

• We **agree** to **accept** this **solution**.

• We **shake** hands.

Indicators

- Discusses and identifies ways to be kind to others.
- Identifies feelings associated with being kind to others.
- Plans and follows through with an act of kindness towards a peer.

The Lesson

Discussion points:

- What does it mean to be kind?
- How can you be kind to other people?
- How does it feel to be kind? How does it feel to be mean?
- How do you feel when someone is kind to you/mean to you?
- Who is kind to you? To whom are you kind?

What to do:

- Brainstorm students' responses to the first two discussion points. Record all responses that demonstrate kind behavior.
- Read through the examples listed on Question 1. Discuss each one and ask students to color the box or leave it blank. Students may suggest some ideas of their own.
- Discuss the third and fourth discussion points. Clarify different feelings—angry, happy, pleased, special, important, lonely, hurt, upset, etc. As students provide their responses, record them in two columns, positive and negative feelings. Talk about which feelings they prefer.
- Students can then think about and draw situations to complete Questions 2 and 3. Encourage each student to think of recent events or one event that really stood out for him/her. Consider how he/she felt during the acts of kindness and color the appropriate face for each statement in Question 4.
- Discuss the final bullet point in the discussion points. This is a good opportunity to point out people who make the students feel good, valued, worthwhile, etc. Students will probably think of people like their parents, a grandparent, or friends. Encourage students to think of other people they may come into contact with who have been kind to them or they have been kind to; e.g., the man who owns the corner store, the next-door neighbor, teachers, etc.
- For Question 5, encourage students to think of someone they normally do not spend a great deal of time with or pay special attention to. Students may need assistance to record their answers for this question.

Answers:

Answers will vary

Additional Activities

- Students can role-play some situations in which they show kind and not-so-kind behavior.
- Write each student's name on a piece of paper and put into a hat. Each student pulls out a name (not his/her own). Students are then responsible for performing at least one act of kindness for that person by the end of the week.
- Display newspaper or magazine articles that demonstrate a caring or kind act within the community. It could be looking after the environment, caring for animals, or working with someone less fortunate.
- Read stories which demonstrate people performing kind and caring acts.

Background Information

Thinking of and doing acts of kindness helps promote a positive, caring atmosphere in a school. Negative acts such as bullying will be less tolerated as "acts of kindness" become second nature.

Students who witness bullying may act in the following ways:

- help the person bullying by joining in.
- help the person bullying by watching, laughing, or shouting encouragement.
- remain completely uninvolved.
- help the person being bullied by telling the person bullying to stop or fetching an adult, etc.

It is important to know that we become caring people over time by doing kind and caring things for others. By being kind and caring toward others, we build good, positive relationships with those people and create a happy and loving environment.

1 Color the ways you could be kind to someone.

use manners	tease them	cooperate with them
think of them	act rudely	be fair
leave them out	be bossy	listen to them
be helpful	not share with them	include them

2 Draw a picture of how you were kind to someone.

3 Draw a picture of how someone was kind to you.

4 Color a face to show …

how you feel when you are kind to someone.

how someone else feels when you are kind to them.

5 (a) Who could you be kind to? _____

(b) What could you do? _____

_____

Indicators

- Completes a news-reporting plan.
- Evaluates listening skills.

The Lesson

Discussion points:

- Are you a good speaker?
- Can people hear you when you talk?
- How can you say what you feel without being aggressive?
- Can the audience understand clearly what you are saying?
- Do you think about what you are going to say before you say it?
- Do you make eye contact with your audience?
- How can you tell if a person is listening to you?
- How can you make it easier for others to listen to you?
- What makes a good listener?

What to do:

- Introduce the activity with a game such as "Telephone" where clear speaking and good listening skills are required.
- Discuss the questions above.
- Read the opening sentences and the instructions for Question 1.
- Students complete the news-reporting plan.
- For Question 2, students listen to a group of students relate their news and complete the plan for one news item they heard.
- The completed plan may be shown to the student who gave the news item or compared with his/her news-reporting plan.
- Students complete Question 3 to rate how well they listened.

Answers:

Answers will vary

Additional Activities

- Students use a similar format to the news-reporting plan to complete daily writing. The sections may be compiled to create a few good sentences.
- Students may practice giving short talks about a topic chosen by you. These talks may be spontaneous or planned.
- Students develop listening skills by drawing pictures according to specific instructions given by the teacher.
- Practice listening skills by playing games such as "Simon Says."
- Discuss characters and actions in books after reading aloud to discover how well students listened.
- Play games such as "Pass the Message."
- Visit an older class to observe a debate or discussion.
- Use a variety of speech patterns to match those of characters from books.

Background Information

Effective communication develops relationships. It allows speakers to get their point across and say how they feel. It is just as important to be an effective listener as it is to be an effective speaker so the correct meaning is given and received.

Speaking effectively can be difficult since children often tend to stray from the point. Giving news, answering questions, and speaking to teachers and friends all help to develop speaking skills. A plan for speaking during news times can encourage students to speak more effectively and enhance writing skills as well.

Effective listening is vital to all aspects of learning and may be developed in a number of ways. Listening to audio tapes and stories, following directions, listening to instructions and news, and repeating messages all help to develop listening skills.

We all need to speak clearly and listen carefully.
This is called "communication."
It helps us to get along better with others.

How well do you speak?

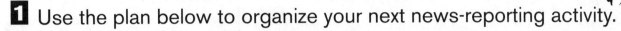

1 Use the plan below to organize your next news-reporting activity.

Who	What	When	Where	Why

How well did you listen?

2 Listen to another student give his/her news.
When he/she has finished, use the plan to write about it.

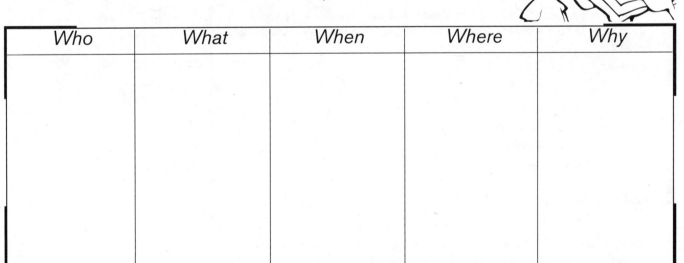

Who	What	When	Where	Why

3 On the scale below, rate your listening skills.

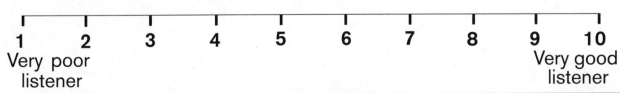

```
1     2     3     4     5     6     7     8     9     10
Very poor                                        Very good
listener                                          listener
```

Indicators

- Identifies information about problem-solving steps from a poem.
- Uses problem-solving steps to solve a problem.

The Lesson

Discussion points:

- Have there been times when you had to make a decision and found it difficult?
- How did you decide what to do?
- Were you happy with your solution to the problem?
- If so, why? If not, why not?
- Are there common steps you or others followed to reach a solution?
- Have there been occasions when you have not been happy with your solutions? What were these problems? Why weren't you happy with the solutions?
- Can some problems be solved by saying "sorry"? What sort of problems?
- Do adults ever say things that hurt other people's feelings? How do they fix these problems?
- What does it mean to "compromise" or "negotiate"?

What to do:

- Discuss the questions above.
- Read the opening sentences and the poem in Question 1. Ensure that all unknown words are explained to the students.
- Discuss the poem and emphasize the questions.
- Students copy the three important questions (What is wrong? What can I do? Can we fix it?) to answer Question 2.
- Read and discuss the scenario in Question 3 with the students and allow them to write their answers. This question may also be done as a whole class group.

Answers:

1. Teacher check
2. (i)   What is wrong?
   (ii) What can I do?
   (iii) Can we fix it?
3. Answers will vary

Additional Activities

- Teach problem-solving strategies through discussion and role-play.
- Orally relate other scenarios where problems exist and encourage students to use the problem-solving steps to solve them.
- Discuss real-life problems and the solutions as they occur.
- Complete and compare problem-solving math activities.
- Think of some "good" problems, such as having to decide between two fun outings with the family.

Background Information

Everyone is different. We do things in different ways, and we often want different things. Sometimes we don't agree with other people and problems are created.

Students encounter problems every day, whether individually or with other students. They should follow these simple rules for solving a problem:

- *Try to solve problems so that everyone wins.*
- *Let people know how you feel.*
- *Listen to how other people feel.*
- *Say "sorry" if you hurt someone's feelings.*
- *Be fair to everyone.*

The basic problem-solving steps are:

- *What is the problem?*
- *What can we do?*
- *Did we fix it?*

As we get older we can learn to look after ourselves by trying to solve our own problems. This can be difficult for both children and adults to do well.

1 Read the poem below.

> I rack my brain. I tear my hair.
> It's hard to cope in the world out there.
> So I put my mind to the test
> To solve my problems to the very best.
> It's not so hard when you know
> That the steps are the same wherever you go.
> What is wrong? What can I do?
> Can we fix it? I can! Can you?

2 What are the three important questions you need to ask yourself when trying to solve a problem? Write them below.

(i) _____

(ii) _____

(iii) _____

3 Read the scenario below and use the steps to solve the problem.

> Natalie has made friends with the new girl in her class. Her best friend, Tina, ignores her when she wants to start a game at lunchtime.

(a) What is wrong? _____

_____

(b) What can they do? _____

_____

(c) Can they fix it? **yes** **no**

Indicators

- Identifies events that cause stress or worry.
- Identifies activities that combat stress and aid relaxation.

The Lesson

Discussion points:

- What does it mean to stress or worry?
- What can you do to help you stop worrying or feeling stressed?
- How do you feel when you are stressed? What does your body do?
- Can all problems be solved? Discuss.
- Who could you talk to if you had a problem?
- What does "relaxation" mean? Why is it important to relax?

What to do:

- Discuss things that could possibly cause students to worry or feel stressed (e.g., arguing with a friend, getting into trouble at school or home, feeling frightened about something). Complete Question 1.
- Discuss some of the ways you could solve the problems students wrote for Question 1. Students write what they did to solve a problem for Question 2.
- Discuss who students could talk to if they had a problem. People may include friends, parents, siblings, grandparents, teachers, the principal, or counselor.
- Discuss the importance of relaxation. You can share his/her relaxation methods with the class. These may include exercise, reading, or working in the garden. Students need to think about what they do to relax and where they do these things. For some students, the only time they really relax may be when they are asleep. Explain the importance of keeping a balance between relaxing and keeping physically fit. Watching TV or playing computer games may be considered relaxation, but it is not a physical activity. Complete Question 3.
- Ask students what makes them feel relaxed. What makes them feel bad or unwell? Read and color the options in the boxes of Question 4. Discuss students' choices.

Answers:

1. – 3. Answers will vary
4. red – getting angry with a friend, telling a lie, feeling tired
   blue – laughing, exercising, reading a book, listening to music, finding a quiet place

Additional Activities

Teach students to relax. Try these calming and stress reduction yoga techniques. (Choose a quiet, carpeted room if possible.)

– Palming Eyes (all ages)
- Sit quietly with the spine straight.
- Rub the palms of the hands together vigorously until warm.
- Place the palms over closed eyes. Feel the warmth and darkness soothe the eyes. Take time to be in this quiet place.

– The Child's Pose (all ages)
- Sit with the buttocks on the heels with the knees together.
- Exhale, bend the body forward and rest the forehead on the floor. Place the arms alongside the body with the palms up. Be as still as a stone resting under the earth.
- Listen and feel your breath going in and out of your body.

Background Information

Mental or emotional health is as important to maintain as physical health. Good mental health involves:

- *feeling good about yourself and your life.*
- *being able to cope with events that occur in your life.*
- *having good self-esteem or being confident.*
- *being able to respond constructively to stress in your life.*

Ways of building positive mental health include doing things you are good at and enjoy.

It is essential children know they don't have to deal with worries and stress on their own. They should talk to someone they trust, someone who will listen, not judge them, and try to understand what is being said. Friends are great to talk to, but sometimes it is probably best to speak to a family member, especially an adult.

When someone feels stressed or worried, physical reactions occur, including a fast heartbeat, tense muscles, a tight stomach, feeling sick, fast breathing, sweating, having difficulty sleeping, or waking up or feeling tired.

1 Draw or write about some things that make you worry or stress.

Me

2 What did you do to solve one of these problems?

_____

_____

Making time to relax and do things that make you feel good about yourself is important.

3 Draw and write about your favorite way to relax.

_____

_____

_____

_____

4 Color things that could make you feel stressed in red. Color things that could make you feel better or relaxed in blue.

reading a book	getting angry with a friend	laughing	feeling tired
exercising	finding a quiet place	listening to music	telling a lie

Indicators

- Identifies what makes him/her different from other people.
- Surveys and records information about his/her friends to show differences.
- Discusses the importance of valuing differences among people.

The Lesson

Discussion points:

- Why do some people look the same and some look different?
- Even if two people look the same, do you think they would be the same in every way? Explain.
- Are you the same as anyone you know? Explain.
- If someone is different from you, are they better or worse than you? Explain.
- What do you think it means to *"be tolerant of other people who are different from you"*?

What to do:

- Write all or some of the following headings listed on the board: Favorite sport, Favorite game to play, Favorite television show, Favorite song, Favorite place, Favorite story, Favorite time of year. Record students' responses. Draw attention to the number of different answers.
- Discuss how students had different favorite things, and even if some things were the same for some people, other things were different.
- Discuss the first three discussion points. It is important that students begin to get the idea that everyone is different in some way. Even identical twins may have different likes, dislikes, favorite things, personalities, fears, etc.
- Read through the statements in Question 1 on the worksheet and ask students to color the appropriate boxes. Once students have colored the boxes, they will have some ideas of their own about what makes them different from everyone else. They can draw or write two of these differences in the boxes provided.
- Students then select three friends and complete the table in Question 3. Some students may require assistance to write the names of their friends. Question 4 requires students to select only one friend to complete the favorites in each category. By completing Questions 3 and 4, students are gathering concrete data showing that everyone is different.
- Students will then be ready to discuss the fourth discussion point. It is important at this stage that students develop the concept that everyone is "equal," which will then lead onto discussion of the final point—tolerance.

Answers:

Answers will vary

Additional Activities

- Students can make prints of their thumbs and fingers to show that every single person has different fingerprints.
- Students draw a picture of a friend and one of themselves. Pay special attention to the differences between the two drawings.
- Read stories which demonstrate differences between people and tolerance of those differences.
- Complete questionnaires that cover other areas to show differences that are not based on the way someone looks; e.g., nationality, family size, daily routines, foods eaten, festivals celebrated, tasks undertaken, etc.

Background Information

Students have the right to be valued for their individuality, including race, gender, culture, and physical and intellectual differences.

We live in a multicultural society. We look different and we live differently. We have different types of families. Differences can enhance our relationships and our society. Students need to be encouraged to recognize, appreciate and tolerate differences.

Tolerance is a skill which can reduce conflict and the need for conflict resolution. It should be an ongoing process. Tolerance is also a quality needed in team building.

Young children may look for basic physical differences such as hair and eye color, or the number of people in the family, types of single-parent families, parents born in a different country, both parents working, or moms and dads with similar jobs.

1 Color the star bursts which make you different.

| I wear glasses. | I'm from another country. | I have a nickname. | I have freckles. |

| I love to draw. | I like to listen to music. | | I can ride a bicycle. |

2 Write or draw two things that make you different.

3 Write the names of three friends. Check the boxes that tell about each friend.

Name	tall	girl	short hair	laughs a lot	freckles	teeth missing

4 Write a favorite thing for you and a friend.

	Me	My Friend
toy		
food		
color		
animal		

Indicator

• Identifies differences and similarities among people.

The Lesson

Discussion points:

• Why do some people look different?

• Why do some people look the same?

• Who was born in the United States? Who was born in another country?

• What foods do you eat that come from another country?

• Are there any traditions/customs that you follow in your family?

• Does different mean better or worse?

• What does tolerance mean?

• Is tolerance important?

What to do:

• Discuss the questions above and record any relevant information on a chart for future use.

• Read and discuss the opening paragraph with the students.

• Students complete drawings of themselves and a friend/family member.

• Students record information about each person to complete the boxes in the activity.

• Discuss similarities and differences and how we are all unique individuals.

• Complete Questions 2 and 3, identifying similarities and differences between the two people.

Answers:

Answers will vary

Additional activities

• Survey the students in the class. Note features like hair color, eye color, height, weight, country of birth, favorite food and music, etc. Discuss the similarities and differences.

• Graph class results for set characteristics (e.g., eye color, height, hair color, foot size). Compare differences.

• Write a poem/story about yourself and then a similar one about your friend. Compare the two.

Background Information

We live in a multicultural society. We all look different. We all live differently. Differences can enhance our relationships and enrich our society. Students need to be taught to recognize, appreciate and tolerate differences.

For children to acquire self-esteem and have unprejudiced attitudes towards others, they need to think of people as individuals, not simply as members of groups with common physical characteristics, customs, etc.

Students should be exposed to people, literature and images that are multicultural and which teach them about other faiths, ethnicities and lifestyles.

Young children may look for basic physical differences such as hair and eye color, or family differences such as the number of people in a family, types of families, whether the parents were born in a different country, whether both parents are working, or jobs that parents have.

People are many different shapes and sizes. They have different colored hair, eyes and skin. People like to do different things. No one is exactly the same.

1 Choose a friend or family member to draw. Draw a picture of yourself below. Fill in the boxes to find out more about each other.

Me

| Hair color | Eye color | Hair color | Eye color |

Things I like about myself

Things I like about myself

Dislikes

Dislikes

Favorite food

Favorite food

Favorite TV shows

Favorite TV shows

2 Write two things that are the same. **3** Write two things that are different.

_____   _____

_____   _____

Indicators

- Identifies what it means to be trustworthy.
- Discusses what it means to be honest.

The Lesson

Discussion points:

- What does it mean to be honest?
- Is lying good or bad? Explain.
- Why do people tell lies?
- Is saying nothing the same as telling a lie?

What to do:

- Read a story about lying. e.g., *Pinocchio,* to the students.
- Discuss the first discussion point with the class and record students' responses on the board or a large sheet of paper.
- Read Question 1 on the worksheet with the students. Discuss their thoughts and direct students to circle the appropriate word to 1(a). For any students who circled "good," ask them to give examples to support their answer. (Some students may suggest a situation where they have pretended to have liked a birthday present in order to be polite. They have told a "white" lie.) Discuss their answers to 1(a) and why they think lying is good or bad. Complete 1(b), giving assistance as required.
- Direct students to look at the situations in Question 2. Discuss what they would do in each situation. Students can write their own responses or respond with assistance if necessary.

Answers:

Answers will vary

Additional Activities

- Read and write stories which highlight being truthful.
- Make colorful posters outlining the three aspects of being trustworthy as outlined in the Background Information (honest, reliable, have courage). Display these around the classroom and school.
- Interview an adult or older person about what he/she thinks about telling lies and/or being honest.

Background Information

It is important to be honest and trustworthy in order to build strong relationships with the people around us.

Honesty is something to be valued. It demonstrates the value we place on ourselves and on our relationships with others.

Being honest is part of being trustworthy. In order to be considered trustworthy, you must be honest, reliable and have courage to do the right thing, even in difficult situations.

1 (a)   Is lying good or bad?   **good** **bad**

(b)   Explain your answer. _____

_____

_____

2 What would you do if each of these things happened to you?

_____

_____

_____

_____

_____

_____

▮ Indicator

- Describes how to care for the environment.

▮ The Lesson

Discussion points:

- What makes up our local environment?
- What things in the environment might affect our health?
- How can we help to care for the environment?
- What is pollution?
- How does cigarette smoking affect our health?

What to do:

- Talk with students about the environment and what makes up their local environment. Include home, school and community facilities and places.

- Have students work in small groups and ask them to decide what things in the local environment can affect their health. Groups can report back to the class and a list can be created from the suggestions. Discuss students' ideas.

- Direct students to the pictures in Question 1 and discuss each situation. Ask the students how these situations affect our health. What can we do to care for the different environments so our health is not affected? Students can write a sentence about each picture to show how their health can be affected.

- Ask students to draw pictures of how they can care for their bedroom and classroom to complete Question 2. Discuss some of the things they might be able to do.

Answers:

Teacher check

▮ Additional Activities

- Ask students to talk with their parents to compile a list of parents' workplaces. Students can decide how their parents' workplaces can be cared for and draw pictures to describe their suggestions.

- Present small groups of students with pictures of different environments. Ask them to suggest ways their environment can be cared for so that it remains healthy.

Background Information

There are many things we can do to care for our environment and keep it clean and safe. Some suggestions include planting trees, riding or walking instead of using the car, keeping places litter-free, recycling, or saving water.

1 Write a sentence about these pictures to show how things in the environment can affect our health.

2 Draw pictures to show how you can care for these places.

Your Bedroom

Your Classroom

FOOD AND EXERCISE DIARY

Name

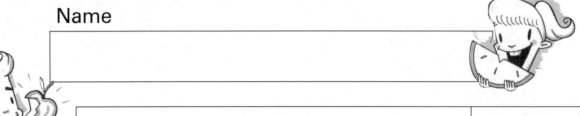

	Food				Exercise
	Breakfast	Lunch	Dinner	Snacks	Type/ Time spent
Monday _____ date					
Tuesday _____ date					
Wednesday _____ date					
Thursday _____ date					
Friday _____ date					
Saturday _____ date					
Sunday _____ date					

A HEALTHY LIFESTYLE

HEALTHY CHOICES

Indicators

- Completes a survey about his/her lifestyle.

- Tallies information from a survey.

- Interprets information from a table.

Teacher information

- Help students to complete the survey in Question 1 by reading each statement aloud and asking the students to indicate if they would be likely or unlikely to do each thing in a typical week in their lives.

- Once the surveys have been completed, ask the class to indicate their answers to each statement through a show of hands. With the students' help, teachers can tally the numbers on the board. The students can then copy this information into the table in Question 2.

- Have the students complete Question 3 independently. Discuss possible reasons for the majority answers in 3 (c); e.g., "Junk food is more tasty than fruit."

Additional activities

- Have pairs of students devise their own simple lifestyle surveys to try out on the class.

- Write a list of healthy class goals based on the results of the survey. Students can report on their success.

Answers

Answers will vary

A HEALTHY LIFESTYLE

Healthy Choices

1. How healthy is your lifestyle? Color *likely* or *unlikely* for each healthy choice.

Eating • I will eat more fruit than junk food.	LIKELY UNLIKELY
Exercising • I will exercise on at least three days.	LIKELY UNLIKELY
Sleeping • I will feel full of energy every morning.	LIKELY UNLIKELY
Relaxing • I will do something relaxing every day.	LIKELY UNLIKELY

2. How healthy are the lifestyles of your class members? Is it likely they will make healthy choices in the week ahead? Tally and total their answers. Include your answers.

	Likely to be healthy		Unlikely to be healthy	
	Tally	Total	Tally	Total
Eating				
Exercising				
Sleeping				
Relaxing				

3. (a) Color the area(s) in which most people were likely to be healthy.

   | eating | exercising | sleeping | relaxing |

   (b) Color the area(s) in which most people were unlikely to be healthy.

   | eating | exercising | sleeping | relaxing |

   (c) Discuss some reasons for these answers.

   HEALTH CHALLENGE

   Write one healthy goal and try to stick to it for a week.

Character Education–Book 1 ©World Teachers Press®

A HEALTHY DIET

WATER AND THE BODY

Indicators

- Reads information about water and the body.
- Completes sentences about water and the body.

Teacher information

- The body of an average adult is between 55 to 75 percent water. Our bodies need a lot of water to function. Each day our body loses up to 12 cups of water (1/2 cup from the soles of our feet, 2 to 4 cups from breathing, 2 to 4 cups from perspiration and 4 to 6 cups in urine). This needs to be replaced.

- Water helps to regulate our body temperature through perspiration, which cools the body.

- When we breathe we take in oxygen and give out carbon dioxide. Our lungs need to be moistened by water.

- The kidneys remove wastes which need to be dissolved in water.

- Water lubricates the joints of our body.

- Water in the spinal cord core helps to support the weight of the upper body.

- Brain tissue is 85% water. The energy in the brain starts to deteriorate if it is not supplied with enough water.

- Dehydration can cause stress and headaches.

- Water is fat-free, cholesterol-free, has no calories, can make you feel full, and is low in sodium.

Additional activities

- Students keep a tally of the number of glasses of water they drink over one day.

- Observe water condensation on a window formed by breathing onto the surface.

- On very hot days, encourage students to keep a water container on their desk and to drink regularly.

Answers

1. (a) Our bodies are mostly made up of water.
   (b) We lose water when we sweat.
   (c) We need to drink at least six glasses of water each day.
   (d) Water helps to digest food.
   (e) Water carries nutrients around the body.
   (f) Water removes waste from the body.
   (g) Water protects some parts of the body from damage.
   (h) Drinking water keeps the body healthy.

A HEALTHY DIET

Water and the Body

A large part of our body is water. It is needed for all the things the body has to do. Every day we lose a lot of water from our bodies by sweating, going to the bathroom and even when we breathe! We can replace this lost water:

- *by drinking six to eight glasses of water each day.*
- *from the foods we eat.*

When it is hot or after exercise we need to drink extra water. We can live for several weeks without food, but we can only survive for a few days without water.

Water helps the body digest food, helps to control the temperature of the body, carries nutrients and oxygen to parts of the body, helps to remove waste, and protects some parts of the body from damage.

Drinking water every day helps to keep the body healthy.

1. Join the beginning of the sentence to the correct ending.

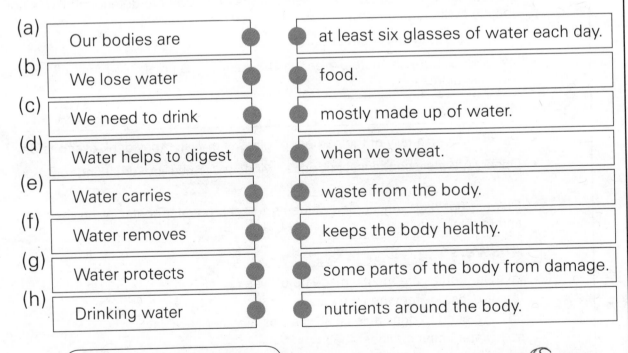

(a) Our bodies are	● ● at least six glasses of water each day.
(b) We lose water	● ● food.
(c) We need to drink	● ● mostly made up of water.
(d) Water helps to digest	● ● when we sweat.
(e) Water carries	● ● waste from the body.
(f) Water removes	● ● keeps the body healthy.
(g) Water protects	● ● some parts of the body from damage.
(h) Drinking water	● ● nutrients around the body.

HEALTH CHALLENGE

Over one day, try to drink six glasses of water! You will go to the bathroom more often but your body will thank you!

Character Education–Book 1   ©World Teachers Press®

WHY DO WE SLEEP?

SELF-MANAGEMENT

Indicators

- Recognizes the importance of sleep in maintaining a healthy lifestyle.
- Identifies if he/she is getting enough sleep.

Teacher information

- Everyone needs to have a regular number of hours of sleep each night as part of maintaining a healthy lifestyle. The times below are average sleep times.

  - New baby .... 16.5 hours
  - 12 months old .... 14.5 hours
  - 2 years old .... 13 hours
  - 5 years old .... 11 hours
  - 10 years old .... 10 hours
  - 16 years old .... 8.5 hours

- When students are having a growth spurt, they may need more sleep than usual because their body is working harder.

- Exercise during the day can help us to sleep. Too much TV or computer games can affect sleep, as can worry.

- Some of the symptoms resulting from lack of sleep outlined on the worksheet can also occur if students eat an inadequate breakfast.

- Read and discuss the information at the top of the page, before students complete Question 1 independently.

- Students may need some assistance to complete the chart in Question 2.

Additional activities

- Students can draw and label pictures of what they look like when they wake up after a good sleep and a bad sleep. These could be developed into posters.

- Discuss why some students may not get to bed as early as they would like, and the reasons why some choose to stay up.

- Read about the life cycles of animals that hibernate in winter and investigate why they sleep so long.

Answers

1. grumpy, yawn, cry, feel tired, can't concentrate, can't be bothered, make mistakes in schoolwork

2. Answers will vary

SELF-MANAGEMENT

Why Do We Sleep?

Did you know that sleeping helps to keep us healthy?
Sleep is important because:

- *we need to rest our bodies.*
- *we need to rest our minds.*

- *our bodies grow and mend themselves during sleep.*
- *a lack of sleep affects the way we work and play.*

Answer the questions.

1. Color the boxes that describe how you feel or what you might do when you don't get enough sleep.

| grumpy | smile a lot | yawn |

| laugh | cry | feel tired |

| can't concentrate |

| can't be bothered |

| have lots of energy |

| make mistakes in schoolwork |

How much sleep do you need?
Everybody is different, but
children your age need about 10
to 11 hours sleep each night.

2. Fill in the chart every day for one week to find out how much sleep you get.

Nights	Times		Hours
Mon		to	
Tue		to	
Wed		to	
Thurs		to	
Fri		to	
Sat		to	
Sun		to	

3. Do you think you get enough sleep each night? | YES | NO |
   Explain why or why not.

_____

_____

HEALTH CHALLENGE

If you find it hard to fall asleep, try reading or looking at an interesting book for a while in bed.

Character Education–Book 1